About the Author

This is my second published book. Writing has always been a passion. I continue to write when I can, whilst working as a solicitor, raising two children and attempting to be the dutiful wife. I find the secret to survival is time with the family, fun with friends and the occasional glass or two of Pinot Grigio! Somehow, that cocktail keeps me going.

What the Chuff?

Nicki Todd

What the Chuff?

Olympia Publishers
London

www.olympiapublishers.com
OLYMPIA PAPERBACK EDITION

A CIP catalogue record for this title is
available from the British Library.

ISBN: 978-1-78830-187-9

This is a work of fiction.
Names, characters, places and incidents originate from the writer's
imagination. Any resemblance to actual persons, living or dead, is purely
coincidental.

First Published in 2018

Olympia Publishers
60 Cannon Street
London
EC4N 6NP

Printed in Great Britain

Dedication

To Amelia and Tristan – do as mummy says, not as mummy does!

Acknowledgments

As always, my love and thanks go to my family and friends, especially my husband, Martin. A special thanks to Jo Booth from Social Media Makes Sense, you've unlocked a door with access to the world.

Thanks to the staff at Olympia for once again investing their time into helping me get my work out there.

Chapter One
April 1988

Dear Sorting Suze,

Help! Something dreadful is happening to me and I don't know what to do. I knew they would come, I was prepared but I didn't expect this. It started with just the one. I shaved it off but then three grew back. They said they would grow in other places, they never said they would grow under my belly button and it's not just that, they are starting to curl. Am I normal? Is there something I can do? Am I turning into a werewolf?

From, I can never wear a bikini again. Wakefield

Dear I can never wear a bikini again,

Fear not. You are not turning into a werewolf. What is happening is perfectly normal. I assume you are a teenager. Your body is changing and will continue to do so. Embrace it. It's a sign you are turning into an adult. Do not shave. More will grow back and then you will be a werewolf.

Here to help as always.

Sorting Suze,

Almost 17 Magazine,

London

What the chuff is wrong with her? That woman. I'm seriously pissed off with my mother. She's horrible when she's ratty. I hate her when she's like this. All I did was ask if I could go to the pictures with Jayne, Richard and Chris. It's no big deal but she said she would have to think about it. What is there to think about? It's not as if I'm going to be home late. I think she's just jealous because she never went out with lads when she was young. I'm fourteen for God's sake; I think that's old enough to go the pictures with boys. I'm not going to talk to her until she says yes.

I go to my bedroom and sit at the window waiting to see if Jayne is in her room. We live opposite and have learnt to sign language quite well after I got bollocked for telephoning her. I wait for about five minutes and then she appears. She puts the thumbs up sign; I wave my thumb from side to side, make a triangle symbol (meaning mum) and point to my head to mean thinking. Jayne puts her hands around her neck. I nod. She waves, I wave back. Suppose I ought to do my homework. I start doing the reading and questions exercise on William the Conqueror. The truth is I don't really give a shit about the Battle of Hastings or that he took the English throne. He's been dead for centuries, why does that matter now? How's that going to help my career in television? I haven't quite decided what I want to do in television yet, I just know I want to work in television, doing something and not fetching tea.

I start doodling on my history book. I practise different ways of writing Jess and Chris. Chris loves Jess, Jess loves Chris. Chris is fit. Chris is mine. There's a knock at my door, in she walks, the commander of my future happiness.

"I've talked to your stepdad and I'll let you go to the pictures provided you let him take you and pick you up."

Awesome. I'm thrash happy. "Thanks, Mum." Get in. This is gonna be it, I'm gonna look so hot that Chris won't be able to resist, and we will be snogging in the back row, my first kiss with my first true love.

I race to the window and wait, willing Jayne to read my mind and come to the window. Nothing. I open the window and make the calling sound of the pigeon, "Cookoo, cookoo," I squawk, my throat is a bit dry so it probably sounds more like the mating call of a toad. Nothing. There is only one thing for it, I'm going to have to make the call. It's a big risk because first, I have to sneak into my mum and Trevor's bedroom to use their phone, I'll never get away using the one downstairs. Next, I need to ensure it only rings three times and then hang up. If anyone answers, it will show up on the itemised bill Trevor gets each month and that will land me in a whole load of deep shit again. Jayne's phone is in their hallway leading to the stairs. It usually takes a good six rings before anyone answers, (we've practised). The chance of someone going up the stairs just as the phone rings is pretty low odds so I should be OK. Jayne knows if the phone rings and stops after three rings, it's me and it means I have news. I come out of my bedroom onto the landing. I'm listening downstairs to see if there is any movement. I can hear the telly is on and it sounds like someone is in the kitchen. Coronation Street is about to start so they won't move from their seats at least until the adverts. I decide to wait until I can hear the intro music playing. When it comes on, I sneak into my mum's room. My hands are a little shaky. It's hard turning the dials on the phone. At first, I dial a five instead of a six so have to start again. The next time I get it right, it rings, one, two, three. Slam. I place the phone down but a little harder than I should. If you put it down quietly it doesn't make any sound. This time though a little 'ding' sound was made. Shit. I am frozen to the spot. Did they hear it downstairs? Did it ding there too? I wait. I don't know what I'm going to do if she comes upstairs. Maybe I should just hide behind their bed? I wait for what seems like forever. It's safe. I move out of their bedroom as fast and quietly as I can. When I get to my room I go straight to the window. Jayne is there. I give her two big thumbs up. She starts dancing. She's doing her Thriller dance. I dance too, I'm not as good as Jayne, I can't do the backwards Michael J moonwalk as well as she can, but I give it a try. She blows a kiss; I catch it and pull it into my chest and wave bye. She really is my best mate. She might be a year, sometimes two years, older than me, but we are best buds. We are going to live together as soon as we can and when we get married we are going to have houses next door to one another. We swore this to one another in a séance we did one night when I was lekking around at her house.

Chapter Two

"Morning Gromit, time for walkies." Urgh. Stupid alarm clock. I hit snooze and instantly go back into a deep sleep. I'm walking along a beach with Chris. He stops and places a flower in my hair, "Come on, Gromit, don't be a lazy bones." I extend my arm and switch it off. I lay there thinking of ways to convince my mum I am too ill to go to school but then I remember, just two more sleeps until the pictures. I have to go to school, she won't let me go to the pictures if I fake another get out of school sickness bug. There'll be no fingers down my throat this morning, oh no. I stretch out my arms and check the clock. Shit sticks, it's seven forty-five a.m. already. Freya will be round in thirty minutes. Annoying Miss Clever Pants, top of the class in everything, Freya. My mum insists I walk to school with her. She won't let me walk with Jayne because we go into different parts of the school, she wants me to walk with Freya because she's in my class. Don't get me wrong, I don't mind Freya, we grew up together. We've known each other since we were six months old apparently. Our families moved into the Barratt estate at the same time and her mum and mine are good friends. We used to have heaps in common; we both loved dolls, playing dress up and 'Let's pretend'. Freya always had to be the teacher, she was/is dead bossy. Her sister, Rachel, was the same. When we played Post Offices, Rachel always had to sit at the head of the table and send orders to Freya and me about what we had to do. We even had to ask to use the toilet, even when we really did need the toilet. We were quite dynamic in our play. Why, we even started making our own newspaper; it was called the Saddle Brooke Sounds. (Saddle Brooke being the name of the street we lived on.) Living on a large Barratt estate meant there was a lot going on. All we had to do was go out like detectives, looking for interesting things to report on. One month we did an article on what type of flowers people were growing in their garden. Freya would often write a piece about our local area and stick on old photos. Rachel would always take control of the front cover. Each month, she insisted on having a 'word of the month' announcement. "This month, the word will be 'Promulgate', meaning issue or publish." I laughed my head off when she wrote on the front cover 'Phlebotomist', as if that's a real word. She reckoned it was a job of some sorts, but I could tell she was just pulling my pudding. My part was to do the joke page. I'd find loads of crazy jokes from my Crazy Joke Book my Auntie Janet had bought me one Christmas. Sometimes I would draw some characters so they would be telling the story of the joke. People loved our paper, or so they said. OK, so it was only made up of about three bits of A4 paper with articles stuck on it with a pritt stick, which we purchased with our pocket money. It cost twenty-five pence, which we thought brought value for money. Our nosey neighbour, Carole, loved it. She loved reading the gossip articles, especially when we announced Mike and Linda Bellamy were expecting their third child.

Problems arose when I turned twelve and decided I didn't want to do that stuff any more. I lost interest in the paper and in playing with Freya. I found myself drawn to boys. I hadn't cared much for them before but suddenly, I found them fascinating. It all started when I watched that Diet Coke advert on the telly. Eleven thirty was on my mind all the time after that. I'd find myself drifting off thinking about that fit man on the construction site. The drifting off at eleven thirty started to become a bit of a problem, especially when I was in my chemistry lesson and set fire to my hair with my Bunsen burner.

My obsession with the eleven thirty a.m. man was how Jayne and I started to become friends. Jayne had moved onto the street a couple of years ago but because she was older, so we didn't hang out. We got chatting one day whilst I was walking into Ossett Town Centre. I'd been sent up to Hillard's by my mum to get some tea bags and a sausage roll each. She said I could keep the change to spend in Ossett Newsagents if I went. Sounded like a good deal to me. As I was walking up the hill to Ossett, Jayne was a few feet in front of me. She had on some wicked purple Doc Marten boots. I'd wanted some of these but my mum said they were too expensive. When she came home with some cheap replica looking ones from Ossett market I had to pretend to be grateful, they've been hidden under my bed ever since, along with the Nikedo trainers she got me.

I was drinking a can of diet coke as I was walking up the hill, listening to my Walkman. I was listening to the Steve Miller Band. Jayne said she could hear it. "Oh god, I love that song, in fact I love that man in the Levi's."

I tried to pretend I didn't know what she was talking about but my stunned expression, like I'd been caught doing something I shouldn't, was written all over my face.

"It's all right," I replied, trying to play it cool. "I'm not much a fan of Levi's," I said, which is a complete lie. I'd actually love some, but my mum says they are too expensive. 'It's only a label,' says my mum. 'I can sew you a red tag on if you like,' she offered. I declined her offer and have cut out the label on the back of my jeans. If anyone saw the Kool Kids label on the back of my jeans I'd be ribbed for weeks.

Jayne started running through her list of top totty. She told me she has a totty board in her room which she does each week.

Every week, she announces her top totty of the week. It's currently Michael J Fox. "So, come on, who's top of your totty board?"

"I don't have one," I reply. Which is true.

"Yeah, but if you did, who would it be?" I think. I'm a bit embarrassed to say. "Come on, I won't tell anyone, cross my heart and hope to die." I eye her curiously. I've never really spoken to her yet here I am about to share my deepest secret with her.

"Well actually, there's a couple," I say, surprised at myself for going further.

"Go on," she says eagerly like I'm about to announce the next winner of the pools.

"Matt Goss and Jordan Knight." I can't believe I've told her; she dragged it out of me. She's nodding. I'm worried. Is she nodding because she's going to tell everyone my big secret?

"I know what you mean, I like Jordan, not much a fan of Bros really but I see the attraction. Anyway, what you going into town for?"

"Got some errands to run for my mum then off to Ossett Newsagents."

"Cool, can I come with you? I want to see if this month's Smash Hits is out." I nod my head, pretending to be cool but actually I'm dead chuffed; I get really embarrassed going anywhere on my own. I promise myself I won't tell her any more of my secrets, especially the one from last night with the rolled up Desperately Seeking Susan poster that I'd stuffed between my legs and felt this weird, very pleasant sensation in my girlie bits.

By the time we got back to our street, we were the best of buds and have barely been apart since other than when we are at school. I'm also now the proud owner of my own totty board.

Matt's name has been at the top of the board for the last three weeks.

I drag myself out of bed. I always like to put on my cassette when I first get up. I pop in Belinda Carlisle and the music blasts out. "We dream, the same dream, we want the same things…" I go into the bathroom, which thankfully is free. Having only one bathroom in the house was never a problem until I turned twelve. Then, like a strike of lightening, it suddenly occurred to me that we should have at least two bathrooms, possibly three, one each. We don't even have a lock on the bathroom door. I mean, what's that all about? What if someone walked in? There are things happening to me that I don't want anyone else to see. Why can't we be like the Cartwright's down the road and knock the fourth bedroom into an en suite? That way, I could use that one as my bathroom and my mum and Trevor can use this one. I suggested it to my mum but she said the same old thing, "Money doesn't grow on trees, Jessica." That might be right but the amount of holidays she and Trevor go on, surely just to miss one would pay for an en suite. It's ever since they started watching that Duty Free programme on the telly, they've been obsessed with Spain. We had Spam, chips and my grandad's home-made pickled onions for a month so they could save up for the flights for another of their long weekends away. As if it's bad enough, we have to eat the same crappy food each night. Grandad's pickled onions really make you fart. The house permanently stinks. For some reason, Trevor's are by far the worst. It smells like a rotting sewer. I never get to go away with them. Mum says it's too expensive for me as they go in school term time. So, Mum's sister, Auntie Janet, comes to stay. Sometimes Uncle Colin comes too but he works away on the rigs a lot so I don't see much of him. Mum says Auntie Janet is glad of the company but all she does is eat all the food in the house and watch television. She's a bit of a bore.

I stand in front of the bathroom mirror. Overnight another huge zit has grown on my face, my left cheek this time. It's all red and swollen. My mum says I should squeeze them but I don't, like, it's disgusting, all that yucky whitey yellow stuff that comes out. It grosses me out. Instead, I just use the special creams that help this sort of thing. It's high-end stuff and really works apparently. The advert on the telly said it clears spots in just seven days. I've been using it for about four months now, but I know it will work. It comes in like a white bottle, which obviously means it's medically proven. I begin to wonder whether, in fact, the colour of the bottle really matters. I mean, if it came in like a black bottle instead, would I have bought it? Definitely not. To make something white means it's clean, sanitary. It will work in time, it's not a con.

I fill up the bath with about an inch of water, grab my soap on a rope Auntie Janet bought me last Christmas. I rub it all around my body and then between my legs. It lingers there a little longer. I have this strange feeling when I place it there. It feels a bit like when I sneeze, a bit of satisfaction. It's the same feeling I had with the Desperately Seeking Susan poster and when I watch the Coke and Levi's advert on the telly. Bang, bang.

"Jessica, hurry up, Freya is here." Crap. I grab my towel and give myself a quick dry. My athlete's foot will never dry up at this rate. I go into my room and start getting dressed. We aren't supposed to wear make up for school but no one notices a bit of blusher, which I apply evenly across my cheekbones. Jayne showed me how to do it. She says it shows boys you are interested. I grab my school books and shove them into my rucksack, and then I turn off my cassette. As I am about to leave my room, Freya is stood in the doorway.

"Wow, you've made some changes," she says, looking around my bedroom. I eye the clock. We've loads of time. I don't know what she is doing here so early. "Has all the Pierrot gone from your room? Even the china doll?"

"Yes," I say, moving the china doll's head with my foot further under my bed.

"So, what made you go purple?"

"I don't know, just like it I guess. I acted on impulse."

"Hmmm," she replies. "And all those posters, what, there must be about one hundred."

"Forty-five actually," and to think she's the genius at maths.

"New Kids on the Block, you really like them?" I nod. "And who's this, Corey who?"

"Haim, from the Lost Boys."

"Never seen it," she replies.

"It's epic, it's based on a true story, apparently."

"Who's this," she asks, pointing to Mike Paton.

"Only the lead singer of Faith No More. Where've you been, the library?" She ignores me. I'm feeling uncomfortable with her in here, it's like she has access to my thoughts and secrets. "Come on, best get going."

Freya seems mesmerised. "Why do you have these?" she asks.

"Because I like to look at them."

"Why?" she asks.

"I don't know, I just do, OK?" Freya looks confused. I'm confused. I don't know why I like looking at these photos of fit blokes, I just do. I don't know why my nipples have swollen to the size of plums or why there is hair growing out of every nook and cranny of my body, it just is. I guide Freya out firmly with my hand and try distracting her by asking about our history homework. This sets her off into one of her bossy teaching modes and gets her down the stairs and out of the door.

Chapter Three

Oh my god, it's Friday. I'm so excited. Pictures tonight. First thing I do when I get out my bed is check the mirror. "Please, please," I pray to the God of Hormonal Teenagers, please don't let me have a zit. I check from side to side then do an air grab; "Yes," zit free. It's like the Gods are smiling down on me. They know tonight is the night. Tonight, Chris will take me in his arms, he will move my hair out of my face and then gently lean in to…

"Here's your cup of tea, we've run out of sugar so I've scraped the top off a tiny tot for you." Bloody Trevor. Always chooses his moments well. Bless him, my mum has him so tightly wrapped around her finger, he daren't put a foot wrong. I mean, scraping the sugar off a tiny tot just so I'd get some sugar. Who does that? It's not like I'm as scary as her.

"Thanks, Trevor," I manage to say, although annoyed he just destroyed my moment. Right, where was I? So, he leans for the kiss, my lips lower towards the back of my hand.

"Frrrrrrrrrppppppp." My mum is stood at the door. "Bloody hell, those pickled onions your Grandad makes could fuel a fire." I stare in disbelief. Is this really happening right now.

"Aww, jeez, Mum. That stinks."

"Sorry, love. Now listen, I might not be back after school; Jan and I are going out for a bite to eat after she finishes work. Not my idea, she insists, she's something to tell me. Trevor will take you in at five thirty and he's going to wait in the car and do his crossword puzzle. Once the film has finished, you come straight home, you hear?" I really want to give an indigent look, but I know if I push it she will cancel the whole thing because that's just how she rolls.

"Can't we even have like a…"

"No. You come straight out and into the car, you hear?" I nod. "You hear me, Jessica, or else we can just cancel this whole thing. Lord knows I ain't that happy about you going, especially with that Jayne, she's been nothing but trouble."

Crapsticks, I need to wind this back or else she will cancel, she's talking herself into doing it even as I stare.

"Mum, it will be fine. I really, really appreciate you letting me do this. I know I have to build trust. I'm so grateful Trevor will take us and pick us up. Don't worry. It's an amazing film apparently, I've been wanting to see it for ages." Please don't ask what it is, please, please. I went too far. I'm racking my brain to try and remember what else is on at the minute.

"Well, Jess, I suppose we have to let you spread your wings at some point but trust me, one step out of line and you won't be seeing daylight until you are thirty."

Boy, that's heavy, for doing what? It's only the bloody pictures for God's sake. What can I do, suck face and spill my popcorn whilst watching Snow White? Get a grip woman. Of course, I don't repeat any of that.

"Yes, Mum. Thank you." I stand up now and give her a kiss. She pulls back, a little surprised; it's been a while since I've shown her any physical affection. I panic again but she embraces me back, slightly firmer and a little more desperate. She leaves.

School drags. Freya is her usual annoying self. "We are having a guess the Kings and Queens of Great Britain game tonight, fancy it? It'll be ace. Last time, Minna thought William the Conqueror was…"

"Can't, have plans. Sorry, sounds like a blast." Freya seems a little taken aback by my curt response or maybe is taken aback by what plans I have. The remaining hours in English Lit seem like forever. I don't hear a thing, except something a horse said to cow, whilst talking to a chicken. The bell finally rings. Awesome. I race home. I'm so frigging giddy right now. I have the evening all planned out. After racing home, I will first have my obligatory poo (I can't poo at school, never could), I always save it for when I get home. I just hope this time I can rush it through. I pick up my Twinkle yearly album from 1982, a particular favourite. Damn it, this is taking longer than I hoped. Twenty minutes later, I am lightened. I've multi-tasked and run the bath whilst sitting on the loo. I hop in and give myself a good scrub. We've no shower. Only the residents who could afford the five bedroom houses got a shower as well. After my bath, I head downstairs and wash my hair in the sink with the nozzle attachment to the taps. It's four forty-five p.m., Trevor is taking us in at five thirty. Phew, I've got plenty of time. I dry my hair with my diffuser. I need to get those tight perm curls bouncing tonight. Once I am satisfied with the bounce of the curl, I then spend some time back combing my fringe and spraying it with hair gel. I can never get it as high as Jayne's. Once it's as hard as it can possibly get, which means I have used most of my L'Oréal Studio spray gel, I start painting my nails black. Just the one hand because on the one hand I am gothic (because I have a pair of Doc Martens (she finally succumbed) and a short tassel skirt) and on the other I'm not. I find it stops any confusion. I apply a little make-up, not too much so my mum notices but enough to show I made an effort. I take a step back in the mirror. Not bad, not bad. I opt for the short tasselled skirt, the frilly white blouse, my black and star print waist jacket, knee high striped socks and my Doc Marten boots. I am hip. I turn off my cassette, no more Bananarama for a while. I check the clock. It's five fifteen. I have some time to spare. I decide to spend the time wisely and sit in

24

front of my mirror, practising my lean in when Chris kisses me for the first time. As I lean forward, I slightly part my lips (because that's what they do on the movies), I then press my lips to the back of the hand and…

"What you doing?"

Crapsticks, she's back. "Nothing," I say, withdrawing my hand from my mouth, grabbing my afro comb and quickly running it through my hair.

"Trevor is just getting the car out of the garage. I'm not sure about that skirt, it's a bit short."

"Aww, for God's sake, Mother, it's fine."

"And those socks, no I don't think so, you are showing too much leg."

"Aww, Mum, come on, I wear this all the time." She's fumbling in my wardrobe, which is really pissing me off. I don't want a fight, I can't afford to have a fight because she might pull the plug on the whole night out. I bet that's why she's doing it. I decide not to create. "Mum, please, I'll wear some tights underneath," I offer.

"Black ones, thick black ones."

"Fine," I say, grabbing the tights from my drawer and forcing them on as quickly as I can. She's still in my room, she's loitering. I don't know what she is looking for.

"Now listen, Trevor will be waiting outside the cinema at eight. I want you to come straight out and into the car. No messing. I mean it, Jess. If you are so much as a minute late you won't be seeing anything other than the four walls of your bedroom for a month." God she's intense. Chill out woman. "You hear me, Jess."

"Loud and clear," I say with a salute.

"And you can stop that backchat right now." I didn't bloody give any backchat. Chuffing hell. This better all be worth it. I make to leave the room. It's now five twenty-five. Jayne will be here any minute.

"Do you want some money?" she asks.

"I'm fine, thanks," I say.

"No, here," she says, offering me three pounds, put this in your bag."

"I'm fine, Mum. I've got enough for the film and to get some popcorn and a drink. I still have some birthday money left over."

"Well, just pop it in your bag, just in case." She's staring intently at my bag. She wants to see what is in it. God, this is awkward. I bet she thinks I've a stash of durex in there or something. I open my bag, recognising I will be going nowhere if I don't do this. She's in there straight away, looking through my bag. Nosey bitch.

"Mum, what you looking for?"

"Nothing," she says. "Nothing, just erm, checking you know, you have everything you need."

"It's the pictures, Mum. What else could I need?" She's eyeing me now and I can smell trouble. I make a quick dash for it. "I can hear Jayne, right, bye." I lean in and kiss her cheek. Big mistake, two kisses in one day what was I thinking? Bollocks. She seems taken aback.

"Stay together," she's saying as I walk down the stairs. She's right behind me. It's unnerving. "Make sure you stay with Jayne all the time, you hear? Toilet together, everywhere together, OK?"

"OK, Mum," I say with a sigh. God help me when I'm old enough to go on my first holiday alone.

As it happens, Jayne is here. She looks awesome. She's wearing her Kicker trainers with the tongue hanging out, some ripped jeans and her favourite rugby shirt. She's tied her hair back in a scrunchy but crimped the loose bits that hang around her face. "Hi," I say, eyeing her not to say too much since my mother is still behind me. Jayne's face says it all. She's excited.

"Hi, Mrs Thompson."

"Hello, dear. Now you two look after one another, you hear? You stay together, OK?"

"Yes," we both say in chorus.

Finally, we are in the car. We are in the back. Trevor pulls out of our driveway. Mum is stood there, waving. She has a look of panic on her face. I swear at one point it looked like she was running towards the car. Get over yourself, woman, it's just the bloody pictures. Oh, and my first kiss.

Trevor drops us right outside the cinema. I can see Chris and Richard in the queue. My heart skips a beat. I'm suddenly really nervous. "Right, well I'm going to just drive around for a bit, maybe grab a paper. So, I'll see you back here at eight, OK?"

"Thanks, Trev," I say. I know exactly where he is going. He's going to put on a bet and go and have a pint. He'll never admit it in case my mother finds out, but Trevor likes to put a sneaky bet on every now and then, whenever he's not under my mother's watchful eye. I don't mind him, I feel quite sorry for him actually. As Jayne and I head towards the cinema, I notice Chris is talking to someone, not Richard. He's talking to another girl. Jayne notices it too. She nudges me.

"Do you know her?" she asks.

"No, never seen her before." As we draw closer, I notice there are two girls. One of them is really pretty and I mean like dead pretty, like Brooke Shields type pretty. What the chuff? This isn't fair. She can't be talking to my Chris.

"Hi," says Jayne as we approach the boys.

"Oh hi," says Richard. Chris is too engrossed in conversation. Richard stops talking to the other girl and starts chatting to Jayne. I stand there looking like a lemon. The pretty girl is giggling at something Chris said. She then looks in my direction. Are they laughing at me?

"Hi, Jess," says Chris.

"Hi, Chris," I say back, trying not to smile from ear to ear but it's hard not, he has that effect on me.

"Hi," says the girl. "I'm Bethany."

"Jessica, Jess, I mean, I'm Jess, not you, that's me. Hi." Fuck. They both stare at me. She does a silly little laugh.

"Well I'm glad we cleared that up," she says laughing, whilst looking at Chris. I look at Chris. God, he looks good. He's wearing some black jeans and a Metallica t-shirt. The queue starts to move forward, they are letting us in. Jayne has managed to wangle her way in next to Richard. I'm kind of stood just outside the queue at the side. When I try to squeeze in, some other girls tighten the gap so I can't get in behind Chris and pretty face. I end up at the back of the queue on my own. I look to see if Jayne can see me. She eventually turns around and sees me. She waves me over but as she does it, she's through the door. I mouth, I'll see her in there, but she's gone, she's inside.

When I finally get through, I can't see them anywhere. I head into screen one to see if they are in there. Thankfully, the lights are still on and I see Richard and Jayne are sat on the back row. They are at the far corner. There is a seat next to them empty, then next to the empty one is Chris and pretty girl. Her mate, not so pretty girl, is sat on the end.

"Jess, I saved you a seat," says Jayne pointing to the seat in the middle, next to her and Chris. I manage to squeeze my way past into the seat. As I walk past Chris, I have a little wobble and almost land on his lap. He puts his arm out to stop me landing on him. God, this is embarrassing. Pretty girl giggles. Chris is trying to keep a straight face. This is all going so horribly wrong. The popcorn trolley comes around as the adverts start. Everyone orders some. Richard buys a giant bucket for him and Jayne to share. Chris and pretty girl get one each but before the first advert has even finished, they've already started a game of throw the popcorn at each other. That was supposed to be my game with Chris, not hers. I buy a bucket and start shovelling large handfuls of popcorn into my mouth.

"Jess, Jess," I turn to look, Chris is talking to me.

"Wefefee," is all I can manage as my gob is full of popcorn, bits fly out as I try to talk.

"I said, have you seen this before?" I quickly try and swallow but the popcorn is dry, I start to choke. He hands me some of his cherry coke. I take a large mouthful.

"Thanks," I say, handing him back the coke, which now has floaty bits of popcorn in it.

"Keep it," he says, smirking. He then whispers something to the pretty girl and she laughs, a lot, it's such a fake laugh, I can so tell. The movie is about to start. As I turn to Jayne, she is already French kissing Richard. His hands are on her tits. I quickly divert my eyes and turn to the other side; Chris is snogging pretty girl. This is crap. I am stuck between two couples sucking face when all I wanted was to suck face with the man I love. Can this get any worse? Before those words even leave my head, I feel something smack my cheek. Some little git from a few rows in front has just catapulted a jelly bean at my face. It really hurt. I can just make him out, he must be about eight. Smack, he does it again. This time I catch him, he sees me glaring at him and sticks out his tongue. Randomly throughout the film, I get the odd jelly bean fired at me. I sit and watch the eighty minute version of Snow White on my own. Not so pretty girl looks equally as pissed off as me. I had no intention of actually watching the bloody film. I thought by the point the wicked witch delivered the apple to Snow White I'd have gone to second base. This sucks.

When the film ends and the lights come on, I stand up immediately. "Come on," I say to Jayne. "We have to go."

"Two minutes," she says as she comes up for air from Richard's lips. I can see the buttons on her top are undone and Richard has slobber on his chin. God, they must have been at it through the whole bloody film. I check my clock, it's one minute to eight. I wait whilst she buttons her top up. I notice Chris is writing his phone number on Bethany's arm.

"I won't wash my arm for a week," I hear her say.

"Oh please, how dumb is that?" I need to get out of here. "Jayne, we have to go."

"What's the rush?" asks Richard. "Is Daddy waiting."

"No, Daddy isn't waiting but Trevor is and he's got to get back as he's going out," I lie. Richard starts to open his mouth but Jayne puts her finger on his lips. She then kisses him and stands up to leave.

"Call me," she says. We leave the cinema. Just as we get outside, Jayne then stops.

"Crap, I've left my coat on my seat."

"Jayne, we are going to be late." It's already 8.05 p.m..

"I'll be two shakes of a lamb's tail," she says and with that she disappears back into the cinema. I stand there not knowing what to do. Should I go with her, should I stay here, should I go tell Trevor? I decide I best just stand here and wait for her, she won't be long. Ten minutes later, Jayne, Richard, Chris, pretty girl and even grumpier not so pretty girl all arrive together. Jayne and Richard have their arms around each other. I'm livid. Jayne can clearly see I'm pissed off. It's eight fifteen, I'm already in heaps of shit. By the time we get to the car, Trevor is looking uncomfortable. We get straight into the back of the car.

"Sorry, Trev, it's all my fault," says Jayne. I look at Jayne. "I left my coat, then had to use the bathroom. Don't blame Jess, it's not her fault." I stare at Jayne, pleased that she's tried to save my neck but still pissed off that she's spent the entire evening making out.

"Well, I guess I can just tell your mum I had to stop for petrol." He looks at me in the rear-view mirror. We both know that won't work. Not in a million years will she believe Trevor would disobey her instructions and do anything other than come straight back. We both know I'm in shit. It's not going to be pretty.

When we pull down the driveway she's already out. She's in her dressing gown. She has de-make-upped and looks scary as fuck. She's tapping her foot. Jayne makes a quick exit out of the car.

"Right, well, er, thanks Trev. See you at school, Jess." She legs it out and up the drive, across the road and straight into her house. I get out of the car, before I can open my mouth she is on me.

"I could not have been clearer, Jessica. I said I wanted you home straight away. What time do you call this, hmmm, what time do you call this?"

"It's…"

"You don't need to tell me the time, I know what time it is. What have you been doing?"

"We, er…"

"I know exactly what you've been doing," she says. She's stood directly in front of me now. "You've been kissing, haven't you?"

"No," I say sharply, insensitive bitch.

"Yes, you have, I can tell, your lips are pink."

"They aren't," I protest. "It's from the cherry cola."

"Rubbish. I can tell you've been kissing a boy. The first time I let you go out and this is how you repay me. Get to your room, I don't want to look at you and don't think you will be going out again because you won't, ever, you hear." I am defeated. I want the ground to swallow me up. I can't be arsed to argue with her. I turn to Trevor. He has a look of sympathy across his face.

"Thanks, Trevor," I say as I head inside and up to my room. I can hear her having a go at him now. Poor Trevor. It wasn't his fault but somehow she will make it his fault. I throw myself on my bed and cry. Then in a fit of rage, I grab my diary and cross out every reference to Jess and Chris. I replace the words 'love' with 'bastard'. Chris is a bastard. How could he rob me of my first kiss? I cry some more. This has been the worst day ever. My heart is broken. I don't think I will ever recover.

Chapter Four

I'm so chuffing excited. It's the yearly summer barbecue party at the Cricket Club down the road from us. Everyone goes, practically the whole street. My mum and Trevor will be there along with Jayne and her folks, Trish and Kevin. It's been a few weeks since the pictures and I am speaking to Jayne again. Not that she knew I wasn't speaking to her, I couldn't risk our friendship over a boy, but in my head, I definitely wasn't speaking to her. Jayne and I have been planning our outfits for ages. I am wearing my denim hot pants with my black body, Doc Marten boots and I've bought a new scarf to tie into my hair. I've also been to Secrets in the Ridings shopping centre and bought some new knickers that have the days of the week on them. They are awesome. Jayne is wearing a short lycra black dress with a white blouse over the top and biker boots. She's dyed her hair red and bought a bright red lipstick from Body Shop. Jayne is hoping Richard will be there, she hasn't really seen him since the pictures, other than at school, they've barely spoken. She wants to go to third base with him. I have seen Chris, but I refuse to acknowledge him. I don't care if he's there or not. Well secretly I hope he is and he sees me looking super-hot and wishes he hadn't kissed that other girl and pleads with me to go out with him but I'm just gonna say, "Whatever, deal with it bro." Unless of course, he really, really begs and says he really sorry and then I might think about it.

Jayne says her cousins are going to the barbecue and her aunt and uncle. I've not met them before, I don't even know how old they are. I wasn't really paying attention when she was telling me because I was checking out the new milk round boy. He calls every Friday night for the milk money. He's a bit older than me, I reckon probably sixteen or seventeen but he's super-hot. I put dibs on him first. When I answered the door to him I was wearing my PJs as I'd just had a bath. I was dead embarrassed, but he said he really liked my Minnie Mouse shorts and top; he said the colour red really suited me. It's not the normal sort of thing I wear to bed these days, but my mum had got me some new clothes from C&A and she said she couldn't resist the because I loved Minnie Mouse so much when I was a kid. To appease her, I wear them, not because it takes me back to being a little girl, no, nothing like that.

It's the Saturday of the barbecue. As planned, I am about to head over to Jayne's house. We are painting each other's nails, toes and hands, then she's going to pin up my hair so it's in a really high pony tail on the top of my head. She's much better at doing hair than me. She's going to wrap my new scarf around it so it drapes down at the back. It's a bit early to do it now but since she has family coming later, her mum has said she can't lek out with me until the barbecue.

My mum is in the lounge. She's in a really good mood. She's got the record player on and is blasting out Xanadu. She's always in a good mood whenever they are going out anywhere, or if they are going on holiday. I like her a bit more when she's like this, she's much more easy going. *"A place, where nobody dared to go, the love we that we came to know, they call it Xanadu..."* Aw, for God's sake mother, shut up, I say to myself, although to be fair, it is one of my favourite songs but she's killing it. She grabs my arm and tries to dance with me. I yank my arm away and glare at her, walking to the kitchen.

"Aw, come on, Jess, we used to sing this together all the time."

"Yeah, when I was eight." She carries on, ignoring me. "I'm off to Jayne's," I shout as I am tying up my Doc Martens. "Mum, MUM," I shout.

"Yes, dear," she says as she twirls up to me.

"I said I'm off to Jayne's."

"OK, love, I'm off upstairs on the sunbed for an hour and then Carol is coming to do my hair. Will you be back for lunch?"

"Probably," I reply, hoping I won't and that I'll have lunch with Jayne.

"Well, I'm making corned beef sandwiches, something to line my, I mean fill us up as we won't be eating until later."

"Don't bother making me any, I'll sort myself out."

She grabs hold of me now. "You need to eat, Jess, you are fading away. Look, there isn't an ounce on you," she says, grabbing my waist and pinching the sides. As I pull away, her hands swipe past my left boob.

"Ouch," I say. She smirks.

"Are your boobs hurting, love?"

"No," I say defensively.

"It's normal you know, love, and don't think I haven't noticed them little bumps that are appearing. You don't need to be embarrassed, sweetheart, it's perfectly normal."

Somebody kill me now. "I'm off," I say, heading for the door as fast as I can.

"We'll go bra shopping soon, darling, and you need some big knickers for when your period starts." Slam. I bang the door shut. Why do I have to have a mother like that? She's so embarrassing. I decide not to think about why I'll need big knickers for when my period starts. I don't want to think about it but I do wonder why she said it. They never mentioned it in the

35

sex ed lesson that you'd need big knickers. Just another thing they didn't tell us about.

I knock when I get to Jayne's house. Her mum, Trish, answers. She ignores me and shouts, "Jayne, Jess is here."

"Hi, Mrs Taylor," I say.

"Hi," she mumbles back. I can never fathom Jayne's mum out. She is either ultra-nice and makes a real fuss or she's borderline aggressive and horrible. Today, she's borderline aggressive and horrible. "Kevin," she practically screams. "You need to wash the windows before they get here."

"I'm on it," shouts back Kevin."

"Hi, Jess," he says as he walks past. "Looking forward to tonight?"

"Yeah, kind of," I reply, playing it super cool.

"Kind of, why kind of…?"

"Leave her alone, Dad. God, you are so embarrassing." Thank God. Jayne is here. She whisks me past her parents, "Quick," she says, marching me upstairs. "They are about to have one of their massive blows, Trish is always such an arse when we have people to stay, I don't know why she bothers." I find it strange Jayne calls her parents by their first name. In fact, there is a lot of strange things I find Jayne does, like for example, she's allowed to stay up as late as she wants, she makes most of her own meals and she is never on a curfew. I wish my mother was as easy going as her parents. As we walk up the stairs to Jayne's room, her older brother, Carl, is stood at the top of the stairs.

"Oooh, hiya girlies, playing with your Barbies?"

"Go forth and die, you nerd," says Jayne. Carl mimics her, repeating what she said but in an annoying voice. I think there is something wrong with Carl, possibly on the autistic spectrum. I've never seen him with any friends, his nose is either permanently in a computer book for his Commodore or he's playing on his electronic chessboard. Trish is always mollycoddling him. She treats him very differently to how she treats Jayne. If there is ever a fight, which happens most days, Trish immediately goes to Carl's defence. I've seen Carl deliberately rip up one of Jayne's pictures she's drawn, and Trish has told Jayne off for leaving it lying around. Kevin is no use. He daren't say anything. However, he does little things for Jayne like leave her little sweets under her pillow and gives her extra cash when Trish isn't looking. It's a strange set up really.

As I walk into Jayne's room I immediately notice her bedroom has changed. Her bunk beds have gone, and she now has a double bed. Next to it is the most amazing dressing table I have ever seen. There are at least eight drawers, four either side, a table mirror with hooks where Jayne's necklaces and earrings hang. Next to the dressing table is a huge ceiling to floor mirror that hangs on the wall. You can see your whole self from every angle in it. Her posters have reduced in number so there's now just Michael Jackson, Madonna and James Dean. Hanging on the wall above her bed is a self-portrait Jayne has drawn of herself. It sort of resembles her but it's quite a dark mysterious painting. It's one of those drawings that's either really good in an arty way that only real artists get or it's total shit. I think it's the former. Jayne is dead good at all this kind of stuff.

"I love your room," I say. I'm so jealous. She's so cool and hip.

"Thanks," she says. I just finished sorting it this morning. Kev bought the furniture for my birthday.

"Isn't that in October?" I ask, looking a little perplexed.

"Yeah, but it's kinda an early birthday present."

"Oh," I add, confirming to myself again that it really is a weird set up here. I don't dwell. We spend the next couple of hours listening to Michael Jackson's Thriller cassette, painting each other's nails multi-coloured with matching toes and Jayne does an amazing job with my hair. I have a huge pony tail on the top of my head with my favourite blue and red spotted scrunchie and new scarf dangling down. She's then backcombed my fringe and sprayed it with gel spray so it stands at least eight inches from my forehead. It looks awesome. I'm trig happy. When Trish bangs on the door that lunch is ready, I take this as my cue to leave. I guess I won't be stopping for lunch. Jayne and I have an excited exchange and agree to meet at the Cricket Club near the space invader games. It gets pretty packed inside and out and neither of us want to be left spending the evening with our parents.

I stand back and look in the mirror. I'm happy. I look amazing, even if I do say so myself. I blow Luke and Jordan a kiss and head downstairs, turning off Chesney Hawkes from my stereo. As I reach the landing, I can hear my mum. She is having a meltdown because her stiletto heel has snapped. We can't leave until it's sorted. She's in her bedroom. As I stick my head around the door, I see there are piles of shoes thrown about the room. She's sat in a heap on the floor. She looks OK I decide, although I think she may have overdone it on the sunbed. "We can't go, Jess. Nothing else matches. I might as well get changed." She looks me up and down but says nothing. I'm not sure if that is a good thing or a bad thing.

"Where's Trevor?" I ask.

"Oh, he's trying to fix my stiletto but it's no use, it's broken. I'm not going, I've nothing to put on my feet. We will have to stay at home." I'm not liking this 'we' thing. I assume she is talking about her and Trevor.

"Well, shall I just go with Jayne, then?" I ask.

"Oh, that's right, just think about yourself why don't you? No, Jessica, you won't just go with Jayne. If I'm not going, none of us are going." Shit pants. This isn't good.

"I'll go check on Trevor, he might have fixed it."

"Whatever," she says as she grabs her wine glass and what looks like a pint of Blue Nun.

I find Trevor in the garage. My mum's stiletto is placed in his vice on his work bench. The heel is firmly secured. "You've fixed it?" I ask with what must have sounded like a huge cheer.

"Hopefully," he says. "Or at least enough to get her down there." He doesn't want to miss it either. It's the only chance he gets to catch up with his dart's buddies. My mum keeps him on a tight leash. She won't let him play at any of the away games so he only gets to play and see his dart's friends about once a month. Living with my mother, I appreciate how he might need more time away. He applies more super glue and I can see out of the side of the heel what looks like a nail. She will notice this. However, Trevor then gets some black masonry paint and delicately paints the nail so it's barely visible. You'd have to closely inspect her stiletto to ever notice it there. After a few minutes, he releases it from the vice.

"That should do it," he says. Then, like Prince Charming, he takes the black stiletto to my mother. I follow. I need this to work. My mother is sat on the bed, pouring herself another Blue Nun.

"May I?" he says to her, holding the stiletto and bending down on one knee. God, I'm going to vomit. I leave the room. I listen closely until I hear a, "Oh, Trevor, you fixed it, you clever, clever man." There is then silence and what sounds like a kiss. Aw, gross. I make a dash for it and head downstairs. Phew, we are back on. Two minutes later, my mum and Trevor are in the kitchen, ready to leave.

"He fixed it, Jess. My hero, my very own Prince Charming."
Yeah, yeah whatever. It feels like a scene from Cinderella where
the shoe actually fit one of the ugly sisters and Prince Charming
looks totally fucked off.

We arrive at the Cricket Club. My mum gives instructions to
Trevor to get her a Babycham and goes sits herself down with
Freya's mum and dad, Jill and Sydney. Freya is there. She is
wearing a slightly oversized party dress with a bow at the back;
even she looks uncomfortable. She's sipping a diet coke. My eyes
gaze about to see if there is anyone I recognise. It's the usual
crowd from the estate. Just as I start to head towards the space
invader games, Freya walks up to me.

"Are you not staying?"

"Yes, why?"

"Oh, sorry, it's just you look like, you know…"

"Like what?"

"Well, like you are not stopping for a party, like you might
be going home, you know, to hang out." Now, I don't like to
consider myself a bitch, but something is boiling inside of me
and I have to let it out.

"Listen, Freya, just because your mother still dresses you up
like a china doll, doesn't mean everyone else has to. I've moved
on, I no longer want to dress up like my Peaches and Cream
Barbie, I don't want to sing into my hair brush any more. It's
called growing up. You should check the term in that thesaurus
you've got stuck up your arse."

At this point, Jayne has joined us. She only caught the latter
end of the conversation but it's enough for her to join in and say,
"Yeah." I feel terrible. I can see the tears welling up in Freya's
eyes. She looks hurt, beyond repair. Crapsticks. I need to try fix
this.

"I just mean, Freya," I say in a softer voice, "I don't like wearing dresses any more." Technically, that is not what I meant. She looks at me. She says nothing. She then takes a turn and runs out of the club, sobbing into her handkerchief.

"God, she's so Gone with the fucking Wind, drama queen," exclaims Jayne. I smile but I didn't really mean to hurt Freya's feelings. I don't know where this venom is coming from.

Trevor walks over and hands me a 7Up and a packet of bacon Wheat Crunchies. As I take a sip, I eye what Jayne is drinking.

"What's that?" I ask, looking at a yellow-looking drink in a pint glass." It looks like a Britvic orange and lemonade.

"It's called a Blastaway."

"What's in it," I ask, looking curiously at her drink and wondering why I don't have something more exciting than a 7Up.

"It's Castaway and Diamond White mixed together. My cousin, Danny, got it for me."

"Is it alcoholic?" I ask with a shrill of excitement. Jayne nods casually, like it's no big deal. God, what is it with her, why do I always feel so inferior? I want a Castaway, or whatever it's called. Jayne can obviously read my thoughts.

"Come on," she says. "I'll ask Dan to get you one."

I follow Jayne over to the table in the corner. There is a large crowd. I make out her mum and Kevin who is sat next to someone who looks almost identical to Jayne's mum and then I remember, Trish is a twin. There are a few other people I don't know, and then I see him. He is sat in the corner talking to another lad, who looks a little younger. My heart thuds. I can't hear anything around me. I can't help but stare. Who is this fit bod before me? He looks up and catches my gaze, or should I say, gawp. He truly is the best looking lad I have ever seen. Move over Matt and

Jordan, you have a rival and this one is in the flesh before me. I realise fit bod is staring back. Jayne nudges me.

"Jess, Jess, this is my Auntie Linda, my Uncle Patrick and my cousins, Dan and Edward."

"Hi," is all I can manage. My eyes are still transfixed on Dan. I am trying to play it cool, my tongue is looking for my straw but it's heading nowhere near. After a few seconds, I realise my tongue has been dangling outside my mouth for longer than socially acceptable. I divert my eyes to my drink and place the straw in my mouth. When I look back up again, I see Dan is still staring at me. Jayne beckons Dan and Edward over.

"Dan, Jess, Jess, Dan, Edward, Jess, Jess, Edward." Edward gives a not interested hello but Dan stares at me a little longer than just a friendly hello. "Dan, can you get Jess a drink?" Jayne asks.

"Course," he says. "What do you want?"

"I, I, I…"

"She wants a Blastaway," says Jayne on my behalf. Dan heads to the bar, he must be eighteen or over. I stare after him. "Easy tiger," says Jayne. "Don't get your hopes on that one, he's bad news." I don't hear her, I am too busy checking Dan's every move to make sure he doesn't leave. I have the weirdest sensation passing through me right now. It's a mixture of excitement, wanting, in fact, desperation. I feel giddy. Before Dan gets back from the bar, Richard joins us. Jayne is all over him like a heat rash. They decide to go outside, leaving me once again stood on my own like a lemon. Edward has disappeared somewhere; I think I vaguely make him out playing pool with Carl.

When Dan returns I am trying to look cool, just hanging about on my own. My body is jiggling a little to the sound of Black Lace's *Superman*. I try to pretend I am watching the young kids on the dance floor doing the moves.

"Careful with this," says Dan as he hands me the pint of Blastaway. "It's not called Blastaway for no reason."

"It's OK," I say, "I've had one before," I lie. Dan eyes me suspiciously.

"Want to get some fresh air?" he asks. Oh boy, calm yourself Jess.

"Sure," I say, perhaps a little too coolly. As we walk outside I can just make out Jayne and Richard near the woods down the cricket field. There are a few people outside, the barbecue is fired up, there are small groups of people huddled about. Dan points to one of the benches. As we start to head over, I hear a familiar voice.

"Jeeesss." Oh crap. It's my mother. "Jeesss." I turn around, knowing that the sound won't go away until I respond.

"Yes," I answer, wishing the ground would swallow me up.

"Me and Trevor are just nipping upstairs to the members only lounge, he's feeling a bit claustrophobic," she slurs. She's pissed which is a good thing. She's far more easy-going.

"Will you be OK?"

"I'm fine, Mother," I say, feeling myself going purple.

"OK, love, you know where we are if you need us." Phew, she's gone. I turn to see if Dan has made a quick exit, but he hasn't. He's still there.

"Parents, great, aren't they?" he says.

"They are a whole breed of their own," I reply. He laughs and sits down at the bench. I take a sip of my Blastaway, perhaps a bit too big a sip, for I nearly spit it out. It's like rocket fuel.

"Strong, isn't it?" says Dan.

"Err, yeah, I must have had a different type last time," I say, try trying to cover up my very obvious lie. I take another sip to try and prove I've done this before; it burns the back of my mouth but I manage to swallow it. Within seconds, a warm feeling passes through my body. I suddenly feel really, really relaxed. Dan takes a sip of his Bud.

"How old are you?" he asks.

"Fifteen," I lie. He looks at me and nods. Jayne is fifteen so he must think I am the same age.

"How old are you?" I ask.

"Seventeen," he replies.

"Are you studying A levels?" I ask, trying to make conversation.

"No, I'm on a YTS scheme. I got kicked out of school last year. I'm working in a garage." Ooh, he's a bad arse. I love it. I take another gulp.

"So, what is there to do around here other than come to this boring shit hole?" I'm a little taken aback. This is like the highlight of the year. The cricket club is the place to go, it's all there is to do, for now until you look old enough to get served in the pubs.

"This is it," I say, pretending to sound equally bored.

"What, there are no pubs in Toss it?" It takes me a minute to work out he means Ossett.

"Well, yeah there are pubs and stuff but you know like, they are up town and it's, er, you know a bit far." I am panicking. I don't want him to leave me to go to the pubs. Worst still, he might ask me to go with him and I know I will never get served. I'm only fourteen. He lays back and stretches his arms out. His arms lay across the back of the bench with one arm behind me. I sit there, frozen, not knowing what to do.

"Relax," he says. "Since this is it, we might as well get comfortable." I take another gulp and lie back, feeling his arm rest against my shoulders. He sidles a little closer towards me. I don't know what to do so I take another gulp of my Blastaway. Now his hand is on my leg.

"Can I just say, I noticed you as soon as you walked in." I snort. I can't help it, like yeah, right you did. "When I saw you talking to the girl with the bow, I wondered what a hot chick like you were doing with someone like that." Oh hello, he really did see me talking to Freya. "I asked Jayne, who's that girl?" and then she came to get me, I think to myself, getting more excited by the second. I take another gulp. His hand is now on my chin, he turns my face to face his.

"It's OK," he says. "I don't bite." I laugh, a slightly hysterical laugh but not in a scared way, in a 'this is blowing my fucking mind,' kind of a way. And then it happens. I am so unprepared, he leans in, parts his lips and closes his eyes. His lips press against me. I sit there frozen.

"Think, think, Jess," I tell myself. I finally remember to part my lips. When I do, his tongue comes soaring through my mouth, wandering around every bit of fleshy, toothy gum there is. We French kiss for what seems like several minutes. Just as I am relaxing into the kiss, I feel his hand move to my chest. I'm not prepared for this. I smack it away. I sense him smile between his kiss. Eventually, he pulls away but stays within inches of my face, or so I feel, I'm not really sure as my eyes are still closed. I blink them open. I'm right, he's there. I look into his eyes. He smiles with his eyes. His big dark mysterious eyes. I don't know what to do now. I never thought this part through. What do you do seconds after your first real kiss? Do you grade it? Give a nod, talk about it? I'm so not clued up on this. I decide to take another gulp of my Blastaway but realise there isn't a gulp left in it. It's all gone. The minute I realise it's all gone, is the minute I start to have some serious room spin going on. Dan removes his arm from around my shoulders and reaches into his pocket. He pulls out a packet of Marlborough cigarettes and offers me one. I shake my head. That would be too many firsts for one night. I sit there saying nothing. I feel strange. My legs feel like lead. I don't think I can stand up. I can't talk, everything feels odd.

"Are you OK?" he asks. I nod. I still can't open my mouth and then it happens. The waft of cigarette smoke drafts past my nose and I feel my stomach flip. I dart to the side and hurl down the side of the bench. The rest then becomes a blur. I hear my mother shouting. Suddenly Jayne is there. I feel Trevor pick me up. There appears to be a lot of commotion. I hurl again as Trevor is trying to move me along. I hear my mother swear as it seems her heel has snapped off again. I don't remember much else except seeing our bathroom floor and hurling some more. I feel like I'm in one of those *Tales of the Unexpected* dramas that's on on a Friday night. It's all a bit surreal. I'm on some kind of fairground ride, possibly the Waltzer. The last thing I remember is my mother pouring pints of water down my throat. I see her sat in the corner of my room on my beanbag as I close my eyes and then nothing. I don't dream, I feel nothing, until the next morning when I wake up. What the chuff has happened to me?

When I open my eyes, I look around the room. I remember the vision of my mum. She's not there. I check the clock. Its 10.24 a.m. Boy, does my head hurt. I lay there a second, trying to take it all in and then it happens; the flash back, the kiss, the vomit, my mother. Oh shit. My hands are covering my face. Oh God, I am so going to be in for it. My bedroom door barges open. Before I even get chance to fake still being asleep, she sees me.

"Well, Jessica, I hope you've slept because I haven't slept a bloody wink. I've been checking on your sorry state every hour to check you haven't choked on your own vomit. What were you thinking?" Oh really, we have to do this now? She's staring at me intently. Before I can even answer, she's off again. "I blame that Jayne, I bet she got you that drink didn't she and where was she, eh? I can't believe she just left you sat there with that boy.

Good job he was a relative of hers or else I would be going round to her house to tear strips off her." Hang on a minute, she hasn't mentioned the kiss, please don't let her have seen that.

"It's a good job I popped out when I did. I wouldn't have wanted you walking into the club for all to see you in that state. Why did you do it, Jess? You are too young for alcohol yet, love." Her tone is much softer which takes me by surprise.

"I, I, I guess I was just curious, Mum. It tasted like pop. I only meant to have a sip, honest I did."

"Yes, well, it's bloody lethal that stuff. That's why I only drink Blue Nun and Babycham. Listen, love, there is plenty of time for all that drinking malarkey, enjoy being a teenager whilst you can. You don't want to grow up too quickly. That nice young man was very concerned about you. It's a good job you weren't sat with a lad who would take advantage, lord knows what could have happened."

"You are right, Mum." Awesome, she didn't see the kiss. "I will leave alcohol well alone, probably forever. It's not nice." I smile sweetly at her, playing the little girl card.

"Well, let's just move past it, shall we? I haven't told anyone on the street you had been drinking. I said it must have been a dodgy burger."

"Of course, Mum. I'm sorry to have worried you." She hugs me.

"I'll get you a nice cup of tea, love. You stay in bed." Bloody hell. I wasn't expecting that. I've dodged a bullet there. I close my eyes now and try and remember every detail of the kiss. Get in, my first kiss and almost second base night. I grab my diary and start writing. Five minutes later, my mum appears at my door with a cup of tea. She doesn't look as happy and then I notice Jayne is stood behind her. She hands me the tea. "I'll leave you two to talk," she says, eyeing Jayne with a warning look.

"God, she's intense," says Jayne. I nod. "So, tell me what happened. Dan won't say a word but you two seemed pretty close by the time I came over. Well, before you upchucked everywhere." I tell Jayne all the details. She confirms he did ask who I was. Jayne gives me a high five, respect for my first kiss, aged fourteen. She then launches into full details of what her and Richard did. Apparently, they went wandering into the woods. He fingered her behind a large oak tree and she had an orgasm. I have no idea what she means by 'orgasm'. I assume she has got her words mixed up and meant she was surrounded by living organisms. Apparently, she then gave Richard a blow job. I've always wondered what one of those actually is. I've never dared ask because I was too embarrassed to admit I don't know. I tried to look it up in the dictionary, but it isn't there.

"It was disgusting. It was all salty, but he really liked it. He said I'm the best he's ever had," explains a proud Jayne. What was salty? I wish I knew what she was taking about.

Jayne stays a little while longer but has to leave as they are having a Sunday dinner before her cousins leave. I blush at the very mention of the word 'cousins'.

Whilst Mum and Trevor were making lunch, I decided I needed to try and find out what a blow job actually involves. I'd once seen a book in my mum's side cabinet called *Karma Sutra*. I'd accidentally come across it looking for some pain killers for her. I'd turned the first page and immediately closed it, being grossed out but now, I was ready to see what else was in there. The book said there are sixty-nine different sexual positions. I have a quick peak, some require me turning the book upside down. Holy shit. I had no idea sex was so aerobic. I was going to need to get fit before I went down that alley. There was no reference to a blow job. I closed the book and slipped it back underneath her books. However, as I lifted one book I noticed a magazine with a woman with her boobs out. I pulled it out. "Vibrations," was the name of the magazine. "Enter and see Candy's blow job marathon," was the caption on the front cover. I quickly search for Candy's blow job marathon. When I finally find the page, there are about fifteen pictures of Candy with different men's penises in her mouth – that is just chuffing gross. I close the magazine. That has to be the most disgusting thing I have ever seen. The more I think about it, the more I feel like I am going to hurl again. I run to the bathroom. Thankfully, there is nothing left inside me to come up. I sit at the side of the toilet contemplating why on earth Jayne would do that? Why would anyone do that? It's just so wrong.

Chapter Five
August 1989

Dear Sorting Suze,

Oh, God. I'm really worried. I'm bleeding out. Does blood grow back? I am losing so much, there will be none left. Is it normal to lose so much on your period? Is there anything I can do to stop it? I've been eating blood oranges as my friend says they help build up your supply. Is that true?

From, Am I dying. Wakefield

Dear Am I dying,

You will be surprised about the actual amount of blood lost in your period. On average it is about an egg cup full. A period is made up of blood and the womb lining. It may look like something from a horror movie but it's perfectly normal, just another sign you are a turning into a woman and your body is getting ready to make babies. However, if you are concerned, you should talk to your doctor. And no, blood does not grow back, and neither can you replace it with blood oranges.

Here to help as always.

Sorting Suze

Almost 17 Magazine,

London

If they can put a man on the moon why can't they find a cure for this hideous thing I have to go through every month. I was dead chuffed when it first arrived. I was in the changing rooms after P.E., as I was getting stripped for the shower, I noticed a small spot of blood in my knickers. I was so happy. I danced around the changing room announcing it to everyone. I now realise why none of the other girls looked impressed. They'd all started their period way before me. I am somewhat of a late developer. I was probably the last girl in my class to start my period. I'm still waiting for my nips to turn into actual boobs as opposed to just plums and I've managed to grow about ten hairs on my tuppence (that's what my gran called it, God rest her soul). Freya has a whole frigging bush. I swear David Bellamy will pop out any minute having found some new specimen of pube lice. They never mentioned in sex ed that having a period will hurt like hell. The cramps are horrific, like I'm properly doubled over. As if that's not bad enough, the amount of blood loss is surreal. I now know why I needed big knickers. Those bloody wedges you have to stick between your legs are massive. When my mum showed me where I had to put it, I thought she was having a laugh. All that for a tiny spot of blood but as the evening progressed, a whole sodding tsunami came flooding out of me. I was surprised the pads would retain it.

I asked my mum about Tampax but she says you've got to have had children to wear them. I find that odd though since some of the girls in my class wear them. One of them is using something called Lillets. She wrote to the company saying what a marvellous product it was and they wrote back thanking her and sent her a free Walkman. I think we should get a free something every month just for having to go through the sodding trauma. Jayne showed me her Tampax. They look like something my grandad smokes. With the amount of blood loss I have, I will be changing it like every three minutes. I decide to listen to my mum for a change and stick with the pad.

I am laid on my bed, waiting for the paracetamol to kick in. I have a hot water bottle laid across my belly but I'm writing lists. Auntie Janet taught me to write lists. She never goes anywhere without a list. Despite feeling like shite, I'm actually really quite giddy. We are going on our first holiday together as family to Cornwall but even better, Jayne has been allowed to come with us to keep me company. I couldn't believe it when my mum told me. Perhaps guilt has set in for all the vacations her and Trevor have taken or maybe she just doesn't trust leaving me alone with Auntie Janet any more, but who cares, I'm off on holiday.

I'm not really sure what to pack for the holiday. I've never been as far south as Cornwall. I've been to Wales a few times in a caravan and it pissed it down most of the time. Since Cornwall is further south (I checked in my atlas book), I wonder if it will be hotter. What do people wear down south? I've watched Baywatch and am assuming/hoping it's something like that. My mum says there is a swimming pool on the caravan site, an indoor heated pool which is just so frigging exciting in itself so I definitely need to take my swimming costume. I suppose I can wear it to the beach if it gets really hot. My mum is taking me shopping at the weekend to go and get some summer gear. She says I need things like shorts and tops. I don't, I need some grapefruit body wash and perfume from the Body Shop, some luscious lips lipstick from Top Shop and a pair of Birkenstocks from Dolcis shoe shop but that won't happen – too expensive, she will say. I will end up with some replica looking things from C&A or from Wakefield market. It's probably best I don't even mention that I want some, that way she won't get the cheaper knock off alternative.

Trevor drops us off in Wakefield on Saturday. We start, as always, at the café at the top of Westgate. It's the one that has the running water down the window pane. It takes me back to my youth. Watching that window was the best thing about a shopping trip with my mum, that and my full fat coke with a twirly straw. Now, there is nothing that excites me about this café. It's full of old people and stinks of grease and cigarette smoke. I don't know why she likes it so much. After handing over my diet coke, I remove the straw and down it, ready to leave. Her coffee sits there, piping hot. She lights up a cigarette, one of her menthol ones (like that makes a difference to the stench), and she does her usual thing of getting out her purse and checking her shopping list (it's definitely a family thing). She runs through the itinerary of shops we need to go to. I hear no mention of the Body Shop, Top Shop or Dolcis. It's C&A, BHS, Woolworths, Boots and the market if she can't get what she wants in C&A or BHS. I'm regretting agreeing to come.

"Jessica, will you not sit there looking like a grumpy hormonal teenager." Rude.

"I'm not grumpy, I'm bored, there is a difference you know. Hormonal maybe but at least I have an excuse, what's your excuse?" Oh, did I really just say that? She leans over the table, her voice has dropped an octave and it oozes venom.

"Listen here, you ungrateful madam, I'm taking you out to buy you some clothes for the holiday I AM taking you on. Unless you want to sit at home for the next two weeks with Auntie Janet, you better buck up your ideas. I'm not having you spoiling MY holiday with your moody, shallow-minded, self-centred, ungrateful outbursts, you hear." Ouch, that stings.

"Loud and clear," I say, wincing a little from the verbal beating. She puffs hard on her cigarette and knocks back her coffee like it's a shot. We sit in silence. I've gone into a full-blown sulking marathon. She will pay for that.

We leave the café, neither of us speaking. She walks a little in front so I have to follow her. I drag my feet behind her. As we get closer to C&A I see she has a spring in her step. She's getting excited. I feel nothing. I hate this shop. Everything she buys me from here I have to cut the label off. The worst is the Clockwise range, they have the logo printed all over the garments. I usually have to wear a large jumper over any t-shirt she gets me, even if it's scorching hot outside. As soon as she enters, she's like a woman possessed, she's straight over to the swimwear section. She starts grabbing things and throwing them over her arms, she darts from one end of the shop to the other as fast as humanly possible. Things are thrown my way to carry. She's gone frantic, it's not as if the shop is closing soon or that someone is going to come in and buy every sodding item on sale.

I can barely see, I have a tower of clothing in my arms. She's slowed down some now, thankfully. Great, let's go to the checkout. I start to head that way.

"Jess, Jessica, where are you going?"

"Over here, I shout." I can't point, I have no hand free.

"We need to try them on, this way." Oh, you've got to be kidding me. She's not kidding. For the next forty-five minutes I am in and out of clothing. I'm forced to turn around, bend down, stand up straight, smile. This is followed with lots of "hmmms" and "what do you think?" Apparently just saying, "it's all right," is not acceptable. I soon realise that if I show some enthusiasm, the ordeal will be over sooner. I nod at her outfits and smile. I even manage a "that looks nice," and "no, it doesn't make your bum look big," (it's looking bloody massive, but I'm not telling her that after her little outburst in the café).

As I come out of the changing room in the denim dungarees, I immediately bump into Felicity Ellis, only the "It" girl from the school. The girl who is always dressed wearing the best of everything. She apparently has a weekly clothing allowance to buy what she pleases.

"Hi, Jess, they look great, very you," says Felicity with a slight smile on her lips.

"They do, don't they," pipes up my mother. I don't know what to say. This girl has barely ever spoken to me. I didn't even realise she knew I existed, except for that one time in P.E. when she whacked me, accidentally apparently, with the hockey stick, straight in the eye. I needed five stitches. Luckily the scar hides under my eyebrow. I contemplate this for a minute. This shop can't be that bad if Felicity Ellis is in here, trying things on. I check out what she is wearing, wondering if I can copy her look when she leaves. I didn't see any of the things she is wearing on the racks and trust me, I've been forced to scour every single damn one. The curtain she is stood in front of suddenly scraps back.

"Oh, Grandma, that's perfect, you will stand out from the crowd." Felicity's grandma walks out of the changing room wearing a dusty pink trouser suit. Her fucking grandma is shopping here. Well, that just says it all. Of course, how silly of me to think Felicity Ellis buys her clothes here. Her dad owns half the new build estates in Ossett. Everything she buys is probably from Dash or River Island. I watch as Felicity's grandma admires herself in the mirror. She then pops back into the dressing room to change back into her clothes.

"I'll see you outside, Gran. I'm going to nip into Secrets," says Felicity.

"OK, dear," replies her gran. Felicity walks past me; I'm still stood lingering in my denim dungarees.

"I had no idea they did clothing for our age group, Jess I always wondered where you got your 'unique' style from. This explains it." She chuckles to herself as she walks off.

"Well, she's lovely, what a kind thing to say. Whip them off and add them to the buy pile," says my clueless mother who is completely unaware that I have just been shat on from a great height. Thank goodness it's the summer holidays and we aren't at school as I know what would be coming.

Two hours later, we leave C&A laden with bags. I'm secretly a little pleased with some of things I have got, in spite of Miss Perfect Pants Felicity. I got another short tasselled skirt and frilly blouse. Also, my red polka short bikini outfit is actually pretty cool but I'm not going to let my mum know I'm pleased. I never want to go through that again.

As we walk through the Ridings Centre, I notice The Body Shop is coming up. I really, really want to get some grapefruit body wash and perfume. I need a plan.

"Shall we stop for another coffee, Mum?" I ask. "My treat." She looks at me surprised.

"Well, that would be lovely but…"

"I just want to say thanks, you know, for the stuff you've bought me."

"Well, that's very sweet of you, Jess. Yes, let's go for a coffee, I can then tick off my list." Of course you can, I think to myself.

One cappuccino, cigarette and coke later, we leave the café. She's in a good mood. I'm a little more upbeat too. As we walk in the direction of The Body Shop, we first reach BHS. She stops. Oh no, not again. She looks inside but doesn't step forward.

"You know, love, I don't think we need to go in there. Didn't you want to go in here?" she asks, pointing in the direction of The Body Shop. My smile must say it all. Five minutes later, I come out with not only the grapefruit body wash and perfume but she even let me get the grapefruit body cream and a new lipstick. Not quite the colour red I wanted, a little more toned down, but it's still super awesome. I'm happy, thrash happy.

The rest of the shopping trip goes by without incident. I don't get any Birkenstocks but that's fine. I still have the plain black flip flops she got me from the market last year. Trevor picks us up and suggests we go to Bella Italia for tea. All in all, it's not been so bad after all. I really am now starting to get ultra-giddy for the holiday. Bring on Cornwall.

Chapter Six

When my mum wakes me up at four a.m., I actually lash out to hit her. I didn't mean to, but sleep is a fundamental part of my make up at present. My hormones are raging in every direction when I'm awake, why wouldn't that be so when I am asleep? If some fucker messes with my sleep, I will actually kill them. Luckily for her, she was outside my range so came out unscathed. Once awake, I was then left with the task of waking up Jayne who was sleeping on the floor at the side of my bed. At first, I poked her with my foot. She stirred a little, grunted but showed no signs of waking up so I went in for the gentle shake. Unlike my mother's gentle shake, I gently shook her arm and whispered, "Jayne, Jayne, it's time to get up. It's our holiday." Her arm flung about like she was swatting away a fly. I went in a little harder with the shake this time. Still nothing. There was nothing for it. My mum was very clear. She wanted us on the road by four thirty hours. Challenging her at this ungodly time of the night/day was not worth it so I did the only thing I could, I went for the full throttle shake.

One blooded nose dried up later, we were setting off on our holiday. We didn't quite make the four thirty departure time. It was nearer to five by the time we left. It's amazing how much blood comes out of your nose when impacted by a fist. Jayne has a pretty good right hook. I was certainly clear about one thing for the future, I wouldn't be waking her up again, EVER.

As good as friends Jayne and I are, we can't communicate at this time in the morning, whether she punched me or not, no friendship can survive the early hours of the morning. We are both sat in the back of Trevor's Mondeo. We have a cushion each which my mum made, in her attempt to try pretty up the car. She wouldn't let Trevor keep his fluffy dice. Instead she replaced it with a dream catcher. We both have our Walkman's on. Jayne is no doubt listening to the Pet Shop Boys since they are her latest band of the month. I am listening to my tape compilation I did last Sunday when the charts were on the radio. I sat through the entire top 40, pressing start and record simultaneously so I could record all my favourite songs. I then took the time to write each record I had recorded on the card bit that sits at the front of my cassette case. I named the cassette 'Epic Cornwall 1989'. I have a great mix from Kylie & Jason, Erasure, The Bangles, New Kids on the Block, the list goes on. It's just a shame that the DJ interrupts the end of every record. I either manage to abruptly stop the record, in anticipation of him talking or I have to listen to a few seconds of his dribble. It really pisses me off when he starts talking early over Richard Marx's, *Right Here Waiting*. It's like my favourite song at the moment. When I listen to it, I imagine Matt Goss coming to our school to do a concert and then spotting me through the crowd. He comes down from the stage, walks through the crowd and comes up to me, still singing in his microphone. He then takes my hand, finishes the song and then we kiss. It's so romantic. I hold that thought until we reach the first of our many stops at the Little Chef. I have never known anyone need to pee as much as my mother. It's so annoying. Perhaps if she didn't drink as much coffee she might not need to pee as much but apparently when she has a cigarette, she likes to have a coffee with it and vice versa. She can't do one without the other and it turns out she smokes about forty a day. That's a lot of chuffing coffee and a lot of chuffing wees!

As we head further south, the scenery starts changing. It's really exciting. It looks nothing like where we live. The roads are more bendy and narrower. It really feels like we are properly away, and this is when Jayne and I start to get giddy. We've already discussed in detail everything we are going to do for weeks but now we are almost there, it means it's really happening. We recap on our lists, as quietly as possible, so my mum and Trevor don't hear. Jayne's list of things she wants to do includes ringing Richard from the phone box almost every evening. In addition to this, she wants to get a tan, finish her Terry Pratchett book called *'Pyramids'*. I looked at the cover but it looks boring to me. She wants to buy a t-shirt from Fat Fanny's and get a matching one for Richard from Fat Willy's, chat up some proper surfing dudes like the ones on Home & Away. She might even snog one if he's really fit and might, just might, go in the sea but it depends how high the waves are; she's barely put her foot in the ocean since she apparently got knocked over by a wave at Bridlington beach when she was five. Apparently, she swallowed some water and was violently sick for about three days. My list includes, getting a tan, chatting up some surfing dudes, definitely snog one and perhaps he might even become my boyfriend and we can send each other letters and speak on the telephone all the time. I digress, back to my list, read my new Judy Bloom book, *It's Not the End of the World*. I was given it by the school for outstanding achievement in my work. It has a special certificate in the front. Three students were selected from each year group and given a book voucher to purchase an educational book. After we had purchased our book, we handed it to the school who then organised a special assembly where the book was presented to you in front of the whole school and parents. OK, so as it turns out, Judy Bloom, *It's Not the End of the World,* is not technically an 'educational' book. I didn't realise all the other boring gits would purchase proper educational books, like *Grey's Anatomy*, *To Kill a Mockingbird*, *Black's Thesaurus*, *Poems of the Decade*, etc. When the head teacher read a sample of each first page, I turned proper red when he started reading my book "...*I don't think I'll ever get married. Why should I? All it does is make you miserable. Just look at Mrs Singer. Last year she was Miss Pace and everybody loved her. I said I'd absolutely die if I didn't get her for sixth grade. But I did – and what happened? She got married over the summer and now she's a witch!*"

Some might argue that it is educational, preparing you for the real world. It probably sets you up better reading stuff like that than learning the poems of the decade. How's that going to help my future? That's what my mum said anyway when she was talking to my teacher.

Anyway, back to my list of things to do. I definitely want to go and see Merlin's Cave in Tintagel. I bet it's dead good. I also want to try some clotted cream. My mum says it's like heaven in a tub. My ultimate aim this holiday though, is to spend as little time with my mum and Trevor as possible. Now that I've turned fifteen, I should be given a little more freedom. Jayne will be sixteen next month. She's sworn that she is going to lose her virginity before she turns sixteen. I'm not sure I want to yet. I want it to be special and so far, there isn't even an opportunity for me to try. Unless of course I make any progress with the milk boy who I have now discovered is called Tom. However, things are going to have to progress pretty quickly if we're going to shag. So far, the extent of our conversation has been around top tips to stop the birds piercing the milk top and drinking the cream. I nodded with genuine interest when he suggested we cut out the cardboard from the egg box. Things need to heat up there if that is ever going to happen. Forgot boiled or scrambled, we need to get those eggs frying.

After our six-hour journey, we eventually pull into the Ocean Wave Caravan Park in Newquay. Jayne and I are practically bouncing off our seats. There are people walking about wearing flip flops in shorts and bikinis. It's like a proper holiday place. You can see the sea and everything. Jayne and I give a high five when we both see two lads, who look a little older than us, carrying surf boards. I was right, this is so going to be 'Epic Cornwall'. We all get out of the car to stretch our legs whilst Trevor goes into the office to check us in and get our caravan key. My mum leaves us to find a toilet. Jayne and I get out of the car. She whips off her jumper, exposing her bikini top. She's so cool. I'd have never thought of wearing my bikini under my jumper. She leans back against the bonnet of the car and places her sunglasses on. I'm not sure what to do. I can't take my jumper off because underneath I am wearing my Fred Flintstone t-shirt. I thought we would be changing first before we went anywhere. I kick some of the grit on the road, trying to look cool. The two lads we saw as we pulled in, walk past.

"All right," one of them says to Jayne.

"All right," she replies. I don't know what to do. I stand there. The other lad looks at me.

"Aye up," I say, goodness knows why. He laughs and keeps on walking. Bollocks. "Aye up?" I never say, "aye up," well, not to lads anyway.

"Shoo, shoo," I hear my mother say. Oh no, don't let it be... but it's not what I think, she is shooing away the sea gulls from her cigarette. Jayne eases herself off the bonnet of the car. I'm half expecting my mum to tell her off, but she doesn't say a word which surprises me. Just then, Trevor walks out of the office with our key.

"Trevor, Trevor, I'd like you to meet Jean," my mum says, grabbing some woman who has just come from the direction of the toilet. "She passed me some toilet paper, didn't you, Jean?"

"There's nothing worse than no toilet paper, ain't that right, Denise," she says to my mum. They both laugh like they have some 'in joke'.

"Hi," says a slightly uncomfortable Trevor.

"Jean and her family arrived yesterday. They are staying in caravan sixty-eight, aren't you, Jean?"

"That's right," says Jean. "It's so lovely here and the evening entertainment, it's just fantastic. Last night it was Magical Morris but don't worry, he's on each Friday."

Oh, thank God for that, I mutter to myself. My mum glares at me.

"Oh, right," says Trevor. "Well we are in caravan thirteen."

"Aww, that's a pity," says my mum.

"Don't worry," says Jean. "We'll see you at the clubhouse. You off tonight?" she asks.

"Oh, definitely," says my mum.

After their final exchanges and promises to meet at the club tonight at eight p.m., we make our way to caravan thirteen. My mum goes in first whilst Jayne and I help Trevor get the bags out of the car. "Awww, Trevor, it's gorgeous. Look, there's a telly and a shower, oh and look at that, they've even put a little welcome pack of toilet paper, washing up liquid and pegs." As I step into the caravan, I'm actually a little impressed. It's much bigger than I thought it was going to be. It has two bedrooms, one with a double bed for my mum and Trevor and the other has two single beds in it. They are narrow, like really narrow, like I will be sleeping on my side type narrow, but it's cosy and Jayne and I don't care because we are best friends.

After we've unpacked, my mum says we need to go and get some food. Trevor says the nearest supermarket is just a five-minute drive away. I look at my mum to try and read any clue that Jayne and I have to go with them.

"Right girls, what are you going to do? I don't want you going to the beach without us but why don't you go for a swim?" Bloody hell. I wasn't expecting that.

"We'll go for a swim," I screech, slightly a little too excited.

"OK, well be at the pool or near the caravan, OK? Don't be wandering too far."

"We won't, Mum," I say, slightly calmer. After her twentieth coffee, they finally leave. Jayne gets out her speakers and attaches them to her Walkman. Out blasts Donna Summer's '*This time I know it's for real*'. We dance about the caravan. Jayne starts doing her professional dance type moves whilst I just kind of jump up and down.

After our five minutes of craziness, we slip on our swimming gear, grab a towel and head to the pool. It's a large pool built in what looks like a massive greenhouse. You can't see in because the windows are all steamed up from the hot air. We can hear kids screeching which isn't a good sign, I just pray it's not full of under tens. I slide open the door and it's not as busy as I thought. The noise just travels. There is a large pool and a smaller pool for the younger children. Surrounding the two pools are sunbeds. On the far side is an ice cream freezer and a counter and, holy shit, wow. I have to double take. Is that actually Matt Goss? Behind the counter is a young man (probably around twentyish), wearing tight red swimming trunks and no top. He has tattoos all over his arms and two on his chest. Oh, my God, he is just drop dead gorgeous. I turn to nudge Jayne, but she's already sauntered over to a sunbed and whipped off her towel. She's laid flat out in her bikini with her shades on, reading *Smash Hits* magazine. I scrape my jaw off the floor and plonk myself down on the sunbed next to Jayne.

"Jayne," I whisper. "Have you checked out the life guard?" Jayne sits up and looks over in the direction of the counter.

"Hmmm, all right but not my type really. You go for it," she says. I find myself thanking her. I'm not really sure why I thank her, it's not like she would pull him over me anyway, I don't think.

I try to play it cool like Jayne and lay on the sun lounger, but the truth is I want to get into the water. I love water, any water. The last pool I had been in was at Dewsbury Swimming Baths which is hardly a match for this awesome pool in a greenhouse. After several minutes of fidgeting, I decide I can't resist any longer.

"I'm going in," I say to Jayne. She doesn't make a move. I wonder if she has her period.

As I stand, I pull my bikini bottoms out of my bum without thinking. Shit. Did he see. I take a sneaky glance over at the counter, but fit bod is busy serving some five-year-old an ice cream. I casually walk over to the deep end of the pool. I want fit bod to watch me dive in. I have always been a great swimmer. OK, so diving is different to swimming but how hard can it be. I know I can do this today. My sitting dive is now perfected. I stand at the end and do some stretches, delaying my time until fit bod is watching. I keep glancing his way. Finally, he has finished with the sprinkles and is back behind the counter. He looks in my direction. This is it. I hold up my arms, bend my knees and lean forward. FLOP. The loudest bang ricochets around the greenhouse. Ouch, my stomach is throbbing. As I come up to the surface, I can see a few bodies around the pool. Jayne is stood there looking furious.

"What the hell, Jess? I'm soaking and so is my mag. What were you doing, trying to empty the pool?" Stood next to Jayne is fit bod.

"You OK?" he asks.

"Yeah, I'm fine," I start, but then realise he's talking to Jayne.

"Yes, it's fine. She was just messing. I'm Jayne," she says.

"Phil," he says taking her hand, staring into her eyes. What the chuff? That's my fit bod. I swim to the edge of the pool and pull myself up. As I lift myself out of the pool some little shit starts laughing and pointing at me.

"Ha ha, look, her boobies are out." Oh crap. My plums are popping out either side of my bikini. Could this get any more embarrassing? I quickly stuff them back in to the cup of my bikini. Jayne and fit bod don't notice. They are too engrossed in talking. I skulk my way back to the sun lounger and wrap my towel around me like it's some kind of defence shield. Fit bod eventually leaves Jayne's side and is back behind his counter. Jayne is glowing. She's picked up.

"Aww, Phil is lovely. He lives about an hour away in Padstow. He's training to be a builder but does this in the summer to earn some extra money. He's a really nice guy you know."

"Great," I say with a hint of sarcasm.

"Aw, come on, Jess, don't be a grump. I can't help he likes me best." Cow, I think to myself. "Anyway, he works in the club on a Friday/Saturday/Sunday as a DJ. He's going to be there tonight. I told him we would see him there." I don't respond, I'm too busy sulking. "And his friend comes with him, who's a pro surfer…" I pick up a little.

"Oh, really," I say. Wow. A real surfer.

"So, I guess we will have to make sure we are both looking super-hot tonight, right?"

"Right," I say with a little more enthusiasm.

"Aww, come on, Jess, I will do you hair and you can borrow my denim cut offs." That does it. I love Jayne's cut off shorts. To make up for stealing my fit bod, Jayne treats me to a Feast. By the time she returns from the counter with Phil, it's half melted but I don't mind, I like the chocolate bit in the middle the best anyway.

When we return to the caravan, my mum and Trevor are outside. Trevor has started the barbecue. As I finish my third hotdog, I realise Jayne has only eaten half a sausage and a corn on the cob. Maybe that's why she has a six pack. I decline the offer of a scone and clotted cream today. I will have one when I've swum at least twenty lengths in the pool.

At seven thirty p.m. we are all dressed up and ready to go to the clubhouse. I can hear the music has started and I am feeling really giddy. Jayne's cut offs look ace on me with my short yellow t-shirt. I try to slip on my Doc Marten boots but my mum stops me.

"No, Jessica, you are not wearing them. It's Cornwall, not the bloody Arctic. Wear your sandals." I look at Jayne's feet. She's got on some black Birkenstocks which go really well with her short black skirt and cut off top. I'm surprised my mum is going to let her out like that, but she doesn't even seem to notice. My mum has completely overdone it. She's wearing the red flowery dress she wore to her friend's fortieth birthday party and has placed a fake clip-on flower in her hair. Trevor is wearing a smart shirt, tucked into his over-the-knee khaki shorts. I imagine it was my mum who insisted he wear socks with his sandals. He looks a proper pillock.

When we arrive at the club, it's heaving. It's full of families. Every seat is taken. As I look around, I notice a woman frantically waving at us from the corner.

"Oh look," says my mum. "It's Jean." We head over to my mum's new friend. She has saved us some seats. Jean introduces us to her family. She has a son and daughter, Rachel and Scott. Rachel looks about ten. Scott is probably about my age. His face is covered in spots and he has a goofy smile that displays his braces. He's what I would describe as a minger.

"Want to go play in the park?" asks Rachel.

"No thanks," I say. Jayne ignores her. We sit down at the end of the table on stools and look around. Trevor gets us a coke each. I can see Jayne is looking for Phil, but the DJ station is empty. The music is playing from their stereo and there is a bunch of young kids on the dance floor dancing to Black Lace's *Agadoo* and *Superman*. I know all the moves as it wasn't that long ago I'd have been up there dancing, but not now. I am so beyond all that kind of stuff.

Jayne and I sit there for a good hour, bored. My mum is slowly getting pissed. I can tell because she is getting louder, and the fake hysterical laugh has come out when Jean's husband, Tony, says anything. Eventually, once the kids leave the dance floor, the lights go a bit darker and from near the stage, "Right, folks," comes a voice from over the microphone. "Get ready to dance the night away with DJ Phil. Time to get yourselves another drink before the bopping commences." I can see my mother is about to bounce out of her seat. God, why does she have to be so embarrassing. Jayne picks up. She's cricking her neck to see if she can see Phil but it's too dark. After a few minutes, The Weather Girls *It's Raining Men* comes on followed by a stream of smoke. Before the street was even the place to go, my mum and Jean have hit the dance floor. I want to crawl into a hole. Thank goodness it is dark in here. My mum then saunters her way over to me, beckoning me to join her. I turn my back on her.

"Come on, Jess," says Jayne, taking me by complete surprise. "Let's dance," she says. She pulls me up. I can't believe what is happening here. It's all right for her, she hasn't got two left feet. Jayne drags me onto the floor and starts twirling about. How come she always look so cool? I see she is twirling towards the DJ station. Now I get it. I'm stood in the middle of the dance floor. I try to edge my way back towards our seats, but my mum and Jean are barricading my exit. Everyone else's seats are up to the dance floor. There is nowhere to go. Jayne has now stopped dancing and is chatting to Phil who has casually removed one of the earphones from his ear so he can talk to her. Crap. I need to do something. I can't just stand here. I do the only dance I know, step step kick to the left, step, step, kick to the right. Three songs later, my mum allows me to get past to get a drink. I sit on my stool, sulking. Jayne has been stood at Phil's side the entire time. She really can be quite selfish sometimes and where's his friend? I can't see any surfer-looking type here. I spend the rest of the evening sat on my own, fending off Scott, who wants me to play pool. As if! Although to be fair, it would help the time pass by. When the bell for last orders rings at eleven fifteen, I give a sigh of relief. My mum comes back to the table. She has sweat dripping from her hair. She looks a right state.

"Jess, tell Jayne we are going." I nod and walk over to the DJ station. The lights have come on now and I can see her sat at the side.

"Jayne, we are going," I say.

"Oh hi, Jess. I've been looking for you." Yeah right, I think to myself. "No, really, I was. Phil's friend, Josh, was here for a bit." Really? I've been sat on my stool all night. Oh, except when I did walk Rachel to the park and push her on the swing, but that was only for ten minutes. "He couldn't stay for long, it was such a shame, I think you two would have got on," she says smiling.

Great. The perfect ending to my crappy evening. Jayne leans in and whispers something to Phil.

"Wait for me outside," he says. "I just need to put away my records. Don't go yet," he says taking hold of Jayne's hand.

Jayne and I head out of the club. My mum and Trevor are saying their goodnights to Jean and Tony and start to head towards the caravan.

Jayne pipes up, "Mrs Thompson, I think I've lost my lucky necklace my dad bought me in the club. Can I go back and check?" No she didn't, I swore I saw it just a few seconds ago around her neck. I check. It's not there but Jayne looks like she's just stuffed something into her pocket.

"Of course, love. Jess, go with Jayne and help her find it. We'll see you back at the caravan." Seriously. She believes her? If I'd have said that she'd know I was up to something. Jayne leads me back into the doorway of the club and waits until my mum is out of sight. Two minutes later, Phil comes out. He takes Jayne's hand and they start walking towards the park.

"Come on," Jayne says to me. I follow them like a lost puppy. I plonk myself on a swing with my back to them as they sit on the bench. I then spend the next five minutes listening to them sucking face. They whisper a little and then I hear a small groan, coming from him I think. There is a strange sound like a slippy sloppy sound and the groaning starts getting louder. I'm not looking, I don't want to know. Well, I do, but I don't want to see. The groaning turns into an "urgh" and the noise stops. I then hear a, "see you tomorrow night, then." There's another kissing sound then nothing. I turn, daring to look. Phil is walking away and Jayne is buttoning up her shorts.

I walk over to Jayne. "What were you doing? What was that noise?" Jayne looks at me.

"You couldn't tell?" I shake my head. "I gave him a wank."

"Really?" I ask. "What did it feel like?"

"It felt a bit like pulling a wet sausage. He fingered me but I didn't have an orgasm. Probably because you were sat there."

"Sorry," I snort.

"Don't worry about it," she says, completely missing the fact that I'm not really sorry. "Come on," she says. "We better get back."

When we get back to the caravan my mum and Trevor aren't to be seen until I hear a, "Is that you Jess?"

"Yes, Mother," I respond.

"Lock the door, dear," she shouts. I then hear some giggling and an, "Oh, Trevor." Aww for fucks sake, I'm not listening to this. I get ready for bed as quickly as humanely possible. By the time I lay in bed, the caravan is rocking slightly but I soon fall asleep, with my pillow stuffed over my head.

I wake up in a crappy mood, having fallen out of the bed more times than I can remember. Why do they make caravan beds so small? In addition to that, the dance of the seagulls at five a.m. this morning, interrupted my already interrupted sleep. I manage to fall asleep again until I wake to the smell of bacon. Mmmmm. Bacon. I check across and Jayne is still asleep. I check the clock. It's nine thirty. God, its early. I try to go back to sleep but the smell of bacon makes me get up. There is something about bacon on holiday, it smells even better.

My mum and Trevor are sitting at the dining table in the caravan with a stash of toast, bacon and egg. My mum looks like shit. She has a glass of water and puts some tablets into it. Clunk, clunk, fizz. Despite looking like shit, she and Trevor are sat like two love-struck teenagers. They are holding hands. I'm going to vomit. I'm not sitting next to them. I grunt a morning to them, grab a plate, stick two slices of toast and three rashers of bacon on my plate with a massive helping of tomato ketchup and go sit in the lounge part of the caravan. I put on the television but am immediately told to turn it down. Bloody woman. As I'm finishing off my last bacon rasher, Jayne appears out of the room.

"Morning, Jayne," says my mum who is beginning to pick up at bit. "We saved you some bacon and egg."

"No, thank you, Mrs Thompson, I'm just going to have a banana and glass of water." Somehow, the bacon suddenly doesn't taste as good. I have the remains of the three rashers chomping around my mouth. When no one is looking, I spit it out of the caravan window. A flurry of seagulls swarm to the spot.

Jayne comes and sits down next to me and whispers, "I can't believe it, I've started my period. I told Phil he could lick me out tonight." I nearly choke. I check to make sure my mum and Trevor haven't heard but they are busy whispering sweet nothings to one another.

"Why would you want him to lick you out anyway?" I whisper back. "Isn't that a bit gross?"

"No, Jess, it's actually really pleasant. Richard did it to me once and I nearly came but he spunked in his new jeans and got in a right strop." I'm shocked. She never told me this. I'm suddenly feeling very inadequate. All I have done is kiss a boy and almost had my boobs felt. I've got some catching up to do.

As if she can read my thoughts, Jayne whispers, "Don't worry, Jayne, Phil says Josh really like brunettes. You'll be able to go to third base with him." I smile. Third base. But then I wonder, is third base him fingering me or me wanking him. I think it's the latter. I'm not ready for fingering yet. I can't see how that will be a turn on.

"Fistral," says my mum. I won't even go into the vision that popped in my head when she says 'Fistral'. "Trevor and I thought we would go to Fistral beach today," announces my mum. It's going to be a scorcher so we may as well make the most of the nice weather when it's here. Plus, Jessy, there are lots of surfers," she says smiling. How the chuff does she know I like surfers and why is she encouraging me. God, I wish I understood this woman; one minute I am not allowed to like boys, the next she's actively encouraging me.

Unusually, there are no objections. In fact, Jayne and I are giddy. My mum insists we take a picnic as it's expensive to buy lunch out. Jayne and I make our favourite sandwiches, peanut butter and chocolate spread sandwiches with a packet of Cheesy Wotsits to stuff in the middle. Jayne's helping of mixture in her Mighty White bread is not as generous as mine. Perhaps I will reduce the number of Wotsits I put in the middle. My mum says that Jayne and I can have a wander around the shops on our own, provided we agree a time limit. Can this get any better? This holiday is awesome.

Fistral beach is amazing. I mean just amazing. There are rocks and cliffs and surfboards everywhere. When I die, I want to come to this place. Almost every other person who passes us is a surfer. It's like bleach blond men were born here. They are everywhere and the smell, it smells of coconut and wax. Arriving at the beach with my mum and Trevor was not quite how I wanted my entrance on this beach to be. My mum in her oversized sun hat barking orders at Trevor who is carrying the windbreak, towels and cool box. Jayne and I stand back slightly. We wait for them to pick their spot, watch Trevor use his mallet to hammer in the windbreak then promptly lay our towels about five rows back. We are within eye range but far enough away so no one knows we are with them. When my mum turns to see where we are, I give her the biggest smile she has ever seen. She falters a little and then lays back on her towel. Awesome.

I laden myself with sun cream, the factor fifty variety that my mum bought me. Jayne is spraying some oil stuff all over herself. It smells great. Within what seems like minutes, I am sure her skin is going a golden brown. Mine looks white, in fact it looks whiter than it did before we got here. I read the label of my sun cream. 'Total block.' Crap. When Jayne suggests we walk down to the sea, despite really, really wanting to be a water babe and all, I refuse. I have to lay out in the sun for at least fifty minutes to start getting a tan. I cannot afford to waste time in the sea. Jayne saunters down to the sea. Her string bikini is really fetching. I lay back, placing my compact mirror under my chin to help direct the sun to my face – I saw someone on a movie do it once.

By the time Jayne comes back from the sea, she has a little following. There are three lads with her. She has been clever and they rejoined her past my mum and Trevor. I now check my compact mirror. I'm going a pinky colour. I don't want pink, I want golden.

"So, Jess, right, let me guess this right. This is Bradley, Alvin and Chad. They are Australian," says Jayne with a massive accentuation on the word "Australian".

"Hiya, I mean, gooday," I say, barely able to speak. It's like the whole of the Baywatch cast has just appeared on my towel.

After thirty minutes of talking with the, who I now refer to as 'Oz's', I realise that despite being gorgeous looking, they really aren't that smart. Every other word is "wicked, radical man, bonzer and fair dinkum". The first fifteen minutes of conversation is fascinating. I am gorging in their looks and enjoying their enthusiasm for all things surf related. The problem arises when you move away from surf talk. It's like their eyes sink into the back of their heads and they turn into these dull looking youths with a mop of yellow/white hair. If you even mention what they might be studying it's followed with an "urm, jeez mate, enough of the questions already." After one hour and fifteen minutes Jayne and I are rapidly losing interest. It's at this point, we agree we should probably go sit with my folks now to have some lunch. The suggestion of parents nearby is enough to see them off and Jayne and I tuck into our speciality sandwiches. Despite trying not to eat the whole packet of Wotsits, is there anyone out there who can actually open a packet of Wotsits and not eat the whole lot?

After lunch, my mum suggests it's time Jayne and I go shopping, especially since I am definitely turning a pinker looking Jess. We need no encouragement. We grab our bags, leave our towels, mags, etc. with my mum and head to the centre of Newquay. There is nothing I don't like about this place. It reeks of holidays. There are souvenir shops everywhere but set amongst it are the most amazing surf shops. When Jayne and I walk through, I really feel as though I belong here. It's like I've found the place I want to grow old in. As we walk down the main street, some guy hands me a leaflet to Dirties Night Club. Wow. He must think I am eighteen. I tuck the leaflet into my pocket. I will find space for this on my wall at home.

Eventually we come across the infamous Fat Willy's shop. Jayne dives in. I wander around. It's great but I'm not sure I want a t-shirt that says Fat Willy's. I'm not quite there yet. I have some spends and I want to spend them wisely. The neighbouring Fat Fanny's doesn't do it for me either. Since Jayne's dad gave her a large sum for spends, she insists on getting two t-shirts made for her and Richard, "He's my Fat Willy," and wait for it… "She's my Fat Fanny." Epic! Whilst Jayne waits for the t-shirts to be printed, I tell her I am going to wander into the shop next door. It's called Rip the Curl Up Dude so I'm assuming it's another surf shop.

I walk in. There is a huge television screen with surfers defying laws of the elements. It can't be possible for someone to glide under a wave like that and pop out the other end, hair still intact, can it? I move amongst the sections, Rip Curl, Quick Silver, O'Neill, Gecko, Billabong. I move through the mixture of bright colours. I'm loving the pink sweatshirt but it costs my entire spends. I pick it up and put it against my torso.

"You're killing that top," I hear from behind me. Crap, I'm not. Jeez, can you not pick the stuff up in here? "I quickly place the top back on the rack. "No, it looks good on you, you really suit the colour pink," says the voice from behind, now grabbing the pink sweatshirt and holding it once again against my torso as I stand in front of the mirror. I look up and see the sweatshirt, I notice the pink colour makes my skin look more of a golden colour after all and then I look up again. Stood behind me is a mop of bleached blond hair, a beautifully structured jawline and the most amazing sparkly blue eyes I have ever seen. It takes me a moment to realise where I am. I swear I can feel his chest against my back and the most amazing sensation runs up and down my body. Holy shit. I need to buy this sweatshirt and him. Can I buy him? I think he realises what is going on and he seems slightly embarrassed that I am now looking at him rather than the sweatshirt.

"I'll buy it," I say.

"Well you know, there is another version in the Gecko range, that's a bit cheaper."

"I want this one," I say, almost a little too needy.

"But you know, it's like a fortune, I mean it's like Rip Curl, you shouldn't buy it unless you, you know really, really want it." At this, his cheeks flush a little. What's this about? I thought that only happened to us girls? Is it a knock off? Is he embarrassed because he's been caught selling cheap knock offs?

"So, I shouldn't buy it here?" I ask. "Because I've seen it in the same shop in the window down the road and it looks identical but maybe you are right, maybe I should buy it from them instead." He looks a bit hurt.

"Hell, no, I mean, erm, no, buy it if you are sure it's what you want. I mean, you look amazing in it, I mean you know, it like really suits you." Can this be happening? Does he actually like me? Just then Jayne walks in.

"What's this?" she asks, grabbing my sweatshirt. I grab it back off her like she's just ripped a major organ out my body that I desperately need.

"I'm buying it," I say. She looks at the label.

"Jeez, Jess, it's like £45.00. I bought two shirts for less than half that."

"I'm buying it," I say, even more determined. I take it up to the counter. Blondy once again is looking sheepish. I can't work it out. Why is he being like this? Jayne spots him and saunters over to the cash desk as he starts to put my sweatshirt through.

"Hi," she casually says.

"Hi," he responds, barely taking any notice. Jayne waits for a minute for him to look at her. He eventually looks up but carries on putting it through the till. He turns to me. "That should be £45.00 but I've added my staff discount so you get it for £37.50."

"Oh, er," says Jayne, walking away from the counter.

"Wow, that's, erm, great, thanks," I say. "But, erm, why?" He shrugs his shoulders.

"And this," he says, handing me a friendship bracelet from the fishbowl sat on the counter. "This is complimentary." I'm stunned. I let him place the bracelet on my wrist and tie it. The feel of his warm hand burns through me in a wanting, needing way. I stare at the bracelet as he finishes tying up the thread. There is nothing else to do. My sweatshirt is paid for, it's in the bag and my bracelet is securely fixed to my wrist but somehow, I can't get any movement in my body to make me walk away. He stands there too, not moving. What is happening. It's at this point, Jayne comes marching over.

"Oh, for God's sake, so we are on Fistral beach, just outside the Wax You Lots cabin. She'll be there," she says, grabbing my arm and physically pulling me from the shop.

When we hit the street, I yank my arm away. "What are you doing?" I snarl, most upset she has pulled me away.

"Oh, please," says Jayne. "We would have been there until like next Saturday if I waited for a move, I just thought I'd help you along." I know she's right but I don't like being manhandled like that. We start walking further down the street, I am just about to enter a shell shop when I feel my arm being pulled again.

"What the…" Oh, I turn, he is stood there.

"I can't make the beach today. I'm working until seven but can I meet you later?"

"I, I'm on holiday with my folks." Something makes me want to be honest. We are staying at the Ocean Wave Caravan Park. I'll be in the clubhouse tonight." He smiles.

"I know where that is. I'll see you there later."

"Bonzer," I say, lord knows why.

"Bonzer," he repeats, smirking.

"I'm Pete," he says.

"Jess," I respond. He walks off, backwards, until he eventually turns, walking back into the shop. I am buzzing. Oh, my God. That actually just happened. I check to see where Jayne is and realise she's in the nearby souvenir shop buying postcards.

"Oh, my God, Jayne, I think I'm in love." Jayne ignores me and carries on looking at postcards. "Did you see him, I mean he's fit right, like top of the charts fit, right?"

"Yeah, he's OK," she says. "Do you think Rich will like this one?" she asks, showing me a postcard of a giant cock. I nod. I'm buzzing right now.

"He's coming down to the club tonight, coming to see me. Can you believe it?"

"Mmmmm," Jayne replies. I don't know what "Mmmmm" means. Perhaps she's just too concerned about Rich, especially since she didn't ring him last night. I won't push it. I help her choose a postcard for Rich and one for her folks. She seems to perk up a bit. We spend the rest of the afternoon on the beach, sat significantly closer to my mum and Trevor having recognised we were the target of a few Oz surfing dudes.

It's quiet when we arrive at the club that night. I'm wearing my favourite nightingale blue dress with my new pink sweatshirt wrapped around my shoulders and my Doc Marten boots. Up my arm, I now have eight friendship bracelets, the top one being the one from Pete. I've not diffused my hair but let it dry naturally. It's a lighter curl and a lighter shade from the sun. My skin has bronzed slightly and I feel pretty good. Jayne is in a mood. She couldn't get her hair to go right tonight and she reckons I've stretched her cut offs. In my opinion, she's put on way too much black eye liner. She looks a bit mean, if I'm honest.

We sit in the same corner we sat in last night. When Trevor returns with the drinks, Jean and Tony arrive with Rachel and Scott. I can tell it's going to be a steadier night as both my mum and Jean are on Britvic 55s. The stereo is playing and the birdie song comes on. My new best pal, Rachel, who is actually eight, comes up to me and asks me to dance with her. For some reason, tonight I don't care. I will dance with her, even if the dance floor is empty. Rach and I do the birdie dance, laughing as we do the moves. I try to encourage Jayne but I may as well have stabbed a dagger through her chest for the look she gives me. At eight thirty, Phil arrives. Not even he looks as fit tonight. His hair is all sweaty and he has grease on his t-shirt. Jayne walks over to him and within what seems like a few minutes, it looks like they are arguing. He puts the first album on, *London Calling* by The Clash.

"What's this shit?" I hear my mum ask. God help that woman. She was playing her air guitar to it last night. I sit back at the table with Rachel. Rachel is practically sat on my knee but I don't mind. I feel so at ease tonight, I'm happy to just go with the flow. Pete will turn up soon and I won't worry about a thing. When it gets to ten, my good mood is evaporating. I find myself snapping at Rachel when she asks if I will push her on the swing. Jayne moves between the DJ station and our seats. She's not happy. She seems slightly on edge herself, but I can't understand why.

When ten thirty hits, my mum calls it. "Right, I think we all need an early night." Poor Trevor had just got his third pint and some scampi fries. He starts sipping as quick as humanely possible.

"I'm tired too, Mrs Thompson," says Jayne somewhat unexpectedly. What the chuff? Since when? Why does everyone want to go home now? Don't they realise Pete is going to show up soon. Don't they realise I'm in love and that if I don't see Pete tonight my heart will shatter into a thousand pieces, unable to ever be put back together. His name is scrolled across the back of my Judy Bloom book.

I try to drag it out as long as I can. Toilet visit, fake cough needing water, I even try losing my favourite friendship bracelet, but my mum doesn't give a shit by now.

"Oh, stop pissing about, Jessica, we are going back. You can make another." Reluctantly, we leave the club. Jayne gives Phil a swift goodbye and heads out of the club with my mum and Trevor. I follow behind, head drooped, practically resting on my foot until I hear "Jess". I turn, can it be? It is. He's here, my Pete, I mean, Pete. At the side of him is some slightly older looking guy who looks like he's wearing a uniform. He runs up to me. My mum, Trevor and Jayne stop in front. I don't care. I need to hear this.

"I'm so sorry, I got stuck in the shop. We were robbed, they took all the cash. I had to wait to give a statement. I told them," he says gesturing to the older guy, "that I had to meet someone. I said I'd only give a statement if he drives me here. The bus doesn't run here after ten." How romantic. I can feel my heart pounding. I don't know what to do. I want to hug him, snog him, pull him to the ground and…"

"Five minutes, Jessica." I look at my mother. "You've got five minutes and then back to the caravan." Wow, a whole five minutes on my own with Pete. I'm ecstatic. I can't believe this is happening. Once my mum, Trevor and a very miserable Jayne are inside the caravan, Pete and I slowly walk towards the caravan. The uniform guy keeps his distance.

"I wanted to see you, to err, you know, make sure the sweater is OK," he said. I smile.

"Well it hasn't complained, I think it likes its new home," I giggle. He smiles and blushes. He can see I'm getting cold, so he pulls off my sweatshirt from over my shoulders. I pull it on and he smiles. Just as my head pops out the hole of the sweatshirt his lips are on mine. We kiss. Not just a quick snog, checking it out but like a proper full on snog that goes on and on. I think we must spend the whole five minutes snogging. I know this because I suddenly hear our caravan door open which pulls me back to reality.

"Jessica," I hear her shout.

"I'm coming," I respond. Pete is stood so close to my face.

"When can I see you again?" he asks.

"I'm here until a week on Saturday, so whenever you like," I reply. He thinks for a bit. I can get here Friday but come see me in the shop first.

"OK," I say. We stare at each other and he kisses me again.

"Jessica," my mother screeches.

"Coming," I say. I reluctantly walk away. He stays stood on the spot, watching me walk back into the caravan. When I am finally inside, I race to my bedroom window. Jayne is already asleep in bed. I open the blind and see he is just walking away from the caravan with the uniform man. Oh my. I'm in love. I know I'm in love. I feel it in every follicle on my body. It takes me ages to fall asleep but when I do, I dream about happy things. This holiday is the best thing that has ever happened to me.

Chapter Seven

Why is it when you find the one true of love of your life, the only thing that will ever make you happy, suddenly becomes such a massive challenge. Our holiday is whizzing by. I suggest each day that we go to the beach in Newquay and that Jayne and I do some shopping, aka, I am going to see Pete in the shop. I turned up the day after the club and was told he was on the later shift. I couldn't come back later as we were having a barbecue with Jean and Tony. The next day my mum insists we go to Padstow for the day, something about the most amazing fish. The day after that, it's raining so my mum insists we stay around the caravan and in the pool on site. This suits Jayne immensely since she and Phil are 'back on'. I'm not even sure what they fell out about it, something about Phil saying how great I looked the other night. They spent last night out the back of the club whilst we watched Doreen's Dagger Show. I didn't need to ask which base she got to this time. She whispered in graphic detail to me whilst we were in bed about how he gave her oral pleasure and she had two orgasms. Apparently, her periods don't last long. I still don't fully understand what an orgasm is but I daren't ask or else I'd look a right div. I guess I will find out one day, it can't be that special. The way Jayne goes on about it you'd think she was describing the effects of a tutti-frutti ice cream. That gives me a warm tingly feeling, especially the fruity bits.

The next time I visit the surf shop I am told Pete has been sent to their other shop in Bude. Before I know it, Friday is upon us. Jayne is uber-excited. She reckons she and Phil are going to go all the way tonight. Which means sex she tells me. I'm glad she clarified because I don't really know what else happens after third base. I've agreed to cover for her. Phil is getting his mate to cover for an hour, so he and Jayne can spend some time together in the back of his Cavalier. If my mum asks where Jayne is, I am to say she is helping out backstage with the little ones' costumes who are putting on a performance tomorrow night for their production of Oceanella (an Ocean Wave twist on Cinderella). However, it is highly unlikely my mum will even notice she is missing. She and her new best friend, Jean, have become the "It" girls on the Ocean Wave Caravan site. Every bored married woman wants to be their pal. They've built up quite a posse. My mum is trying to play it ultra-cool. When I asked if Jayne and I could go hang out at the park for a bit, she said, "Whatever". It's just so embarrassing to have a mother like that. In a lot of ways, I wish she was the same old dragon like she is at home. However, we wouldn't have this freedom so I just have to endure her desperate attempt to relive her youth.

I make a special effort tonight. I'm wearing my ruffled white blouse with my new tasselled skirt, with, of course, my special surfing pink jumper fastened over my shoulders, even if it is too warm and my Doc Marten boots. Jayne has tied my hair up into a really high pony tail on the top of my head and I am wearing my almost-red lipstick from the Body Shop. Even Trevor said I look, "OK". Jayne has on her black leather trousers and see through blouse. I am gobsmacked my mother says nothing about it. You can see her black bra straight through it. Jayne shows me the packet of condoms she has in her bumbag. Apparently, she has been carrying them around for the last six months. I wonder if I should have some in my bumbag but then I would never buy any from the pharmacy. Mr Clancey knows my mum really well and he would definitely tell her. The only other place to get them is from the men's toilet machine in the pub. I only know they are in there because Christian Draper was bragging about it at school.

When we arrive at the club, all is going to plan. Jayne and I are left to sit in the corner on the opposite side of the room from my mum and Jean and their posse. When no one is looking, Jayne and Phil sneak off. I make sure Rachel is sitting with me with her back turned so should my mum glance over, she will see a body but not be able to make out who it is due to the darkness in the club. We are on a marathon Uno run. The only problem I will have is if Mum starts dancing, she may saunter over. However, given I can hear her fake laugh echoing around the room, over the music, I am assuming she is enjoying her conversation. Trevor pops over every now and then to offer to buy us a drink. I'm not sure whether he has twigged it's Rachel and not Jayne sat with me, but he doesn't say anything. I don't think he wants to rock the boat.

It's nine fifteen. Jayne has been gone about thirty minutes. I'm not expecting to see her for about another half an hour so when she comes stomping through the front door, make-up running down her face with a bloody mouth, I'm a little taken aback.

"What happened?" I ask as she throws herself down in a heap on the chair. I rush to the bar and grab some ice to wrap in the bar towel I have just nicked. I hand her the towel and she presses it against her lip.

"Well it turns out Mr Fucking DJ Phil has a girlfriend."

"Ooh," is all I can manage in reply.

"Apparently, she's been spying on us the whole time."

"Right," I say, concerned.

"The dirty bitch waited right up until my trousers and pants were off before she came over and dragged me out of the car by my leg." I suggest to Rachel she might want to go find her brother for a bit.

"And what did he do," I ask, feeling mortified for my friend.

"He tried to reason with her, the cock. Told her it wasn't what it looked like."

"So, then what happened."

"So then she starts yelling at me, saying it's all my fault and that I'm cheap."

"What did you do?"

"I punched her in the face." Oh crap, I think to myself. Does this mean the police might be here soon?

"But why are you bleeding?"

"I'm not, I punched Phil, too. His lip bust and splattered on me. It's his blood, not mine," she says, handing the towel back. Shit. This isn't good. They might get us kicked off the site. Holy crap, can you imagine if that happened. What would my mother say? It's not even worth thinking about. What I do know is that we need to get out of here and fast.

"I think we should go back to the caravan," I find myself saying. Jayne is sobbing now.

"And to think I let him come in my mouth." Come where, I wonder but I haven't the time to think any more about that. I walk over to my mum who is definitely now three sheets to the wind.

"Jayne isn't feeling well, I lie. We are going to go back to the caravan."

It's at this point I wonder if my mum is going to kick into parent mode and insist on coming back with us but all I get back is, "OK, love. Look after her and each other. You know where we are if you need us."

"Thanks," I say.

Trevor then grabs my hand. "Is she OK?" he asks. He knows there is more to this.

"She's fine," I say. "She just has a really bad headache."

"Any bother, Jess, and you come and get me, OK?"

"Sure," I say, trying to play it down when secretly I am thinking we are going to be arrested or jumped on as soon as we step out of the club.

When we walk out, I check every angle to make sure no one is waiting for us.

"Come on, Jayne, quick, let's go," I shout. Jayne saunters down towards the caravan. She doesn't seem concerned at all. I must look like some kind of ninja dancing in the shadows.

As we near our caravan, I can almost make a sigh of relief until I hear in a Brummie accent, "Hi, my name's Simon, that's Chad and that's Jason. Wanna come in for a smoke?" I look behind me and there are three boys' heads poking out of a caravan window.

"No," I say, still playing at dancing ninja.

"Sure," says Jayne, who is now wiping away the make-up from under her eyes.

"Jayne, we need to get back to the caravan, what if the…?"

"What if the what, Jess? Can't you see I am traumatised? This will take my mind off it." I don't believe her. One minute she is heartbroken, the next she is positively beaming. The truth is, in the back of mind, I am thinking about Pete. If he doesn't see me at the club, he knows where my caravan is. I am certain he will come there, especially since I pointed out my bedroom window. I need us to get back there. Jayne can see I am not happy.

"Five minutes, Jess, I promise. Just five minutes and then we head back, OK?"

"OK," I reluctantly agree. It's nine thirty. At the very latest, we will be back at the caravan at ten p.m. I know it's likely Pete won't arrive until later anyway so that should work out fine.

At ten thirty we finally leave the caravan. Jayne is buzzing. I never knew she smoked but the way she puffed on that Benson & Hedges was like a proper pro. I declined. I didn't want my breath to be all smoky for when Pete showed up. Jayne and Simon hit it off. There was some serious flirting going on. Apparently, they had just arrived that day from Birmingham. They were all eighteen and staying in the caravan on their own. I felt really uncomfortable with them but Jayne was in her element. I only managed to pull her away when I suggested we all meet at Fistral Beach tomorrow. That did the trick.

As we arrive at our caravan, I breathe a sigh of relief that the lights aren't on. Phew. My mother isn't back wondering where the hell we are. I am not worried though as I swear I can hear her faint dulcet tone singing to Xanadu. I walk in first and put on all the lights. I boil the kettle to make a cup of tea. Jayne reaches down into the fridge and pulls out one of Trevor's beers. Then she stands up.

"What's this?" she asks, holding a white piece of paper. She reads:

Jess, I am sorry I haven't seen you this week. The shop told me you had been in. I rushed over as soon as I could. I saw your folks in the club and hung about for a bit. I couldn't stay long as I got a lift here and had to go. I'm sorry not to see you... Pete

I want to cry. Actually, I want to run out of this caravan and run all the way to wherever it is Pete might be. How can this be happening to me?

"Aww, that's a shame, you missed Pete." I look at Jayne. It's her fault I missed Pete. She made us go into the caravan because I felt sorry for her. Now here she is with boyfriend number three and look where I am. I feel a rage building inside me. I really just want to tell her to fuck off but before I get chance to say anything, "Night," she says as she wanders into our bedroom with her bottle of beer. I throw myself onto the settee and cry. A little while later, I am woken up by the door opening.

"Aww, Trevor, look. She's waited up for us," slurs my mother.

"Everything OK, Jess?" asks a concerned Trevor. I nod. I can't speak. I wander into the bedroom and shut the door behind me. Jayne is asleep with her Walkman on. Her bottle of beer is empty so I throw it outside the caravan window in case my mum should see it in the morning and think it's mine. I climb into bed and have a little bit more of a cry. Then I come up with a plan. No matter what happens, tomorrow I am going to the shop and will sit outside all day until Pete arrives and Jayne can just suck it up. She owes me this.

Of course, I do just that. My mum is too hungover to argue and wants a day at the beach and Jayne can tell I mean business today. She can see Simon later. By three p.m. the nice girl from the shop comes out and talks to me.

"Hey dudette, you're Pete's friend, right? I nod. "You waiting for him?" she asks. I nod again. Jayne sighs.

"Sorry, chick, but he's off this week. Gone to the city with his folks. He's back Saturday."

"Thanks," I manage. Jayne puts her arm around me.

"Aww, never mind, Jess. It just wasn't meant to be. Listen, Simon says that Chad is really into you. You know you two should get it on." I say nothing. I can't think about Chad right now. My heart is breaking – again. How can love be so cruel.

The last week trickles by. I really want it to be over. Watching Jayne and Simon play a loved-up couple sickens me, especially when Jayne is deliberately being over familiar with Simon right in front of Phil, whose lip is still slightly swollen.

My mother and her gathering continue to be loud and drunk for the rest of the week. By the time Thursday comes, I am all packed up ready to go home. My mum and Jayne both seem in denial that we are leaving soon.

"Oh, Trevor," she sighs. "This has been the best damn holiday ever, don't you think?"

"Yes, dear," replies Trevor, who looks knackered. Whilst I think he might have enjoyed my mother's affection (makes me vomit in my mouth just thinking about it), I feel his wallet is slightly lighter and he's not used to this kind of a social life. Jayne says that she and Simon have agreed they are going to meet up when she is home. Something about a hotel somewhere between Ossett and Birmingham. I'm not quite sure where that will be, Sheffield perhaps? However, in spite of that, she tells me how much she is looking forward to seeing Richard and how she has missed him. She has told him there is only one phone box on site and that it gets broken almost every night by the kids staying here. That's why she has only rung him twice. Whatever, I think. I don't care for Richard or Simon right now. In fact, I am definitely off boys for good.

On our last night, my mother insists we all get dressed up and head to the club. Jayne needs no encouragement and puts on her leather trousers again and see through top. I can't be arsed so stick on my denim dungarees and wear my pink jumper. I make no effort with my hair or make up. I'm going au naturel tonight. We arrive, as always, to my mother's posse. I insist on going to the bar by myself whilst Jayne secures our seats in the corner. Simon is already there waiting. Chad and Jason have gone into downtown Newquay.

I order two cokes and ask for a bag of scampi fries. "That'll pong a bit," comes a voice from behind me. I turn and there he is, Pete. I have to double take. Is that really him. My Pete. He is stood there smiling. I want to throw my arms around him but manage to control myself.

"It's you," is all I can manage.

"It's you," he says back. "Mind if I join you?" he asks. I don't reply. I am staring at his face; his blond streaked hair is in his eyes and his sparkly blue eyes are peeping out between the strands. He is wearing the same make jumper as me, except his is powder blue. He has cut off beneath the knee shorts and is wearing flip flops. I bloody love surfers. We walk over to the table in silence. Jayne and Simon detangle themselves from one another as I announce, "It's my Pete." I feel my face go pink. I didn't mean "my Pete."

"Hi," says Pete. "I'm Jess's Pete." I must be violet now. We sit down still not speaking a word.

"All right," says Simon and then turns his attention back to Jayne and is sticking his hand down her top which Jayne finds hilarious.

"Hi, Pete," giggles Jayne. "I'm glad you are here. Jess can stop being a moody cow now." Bitch, I think to myself. OK so I may have been counting down the seconds until we leave here but she didn't need to say that.

Pete starts telling me about his week. It turns out his parents have a flat in London which belonged to Pete's grandmother and got passed to his dad when she died. In the summer holidays they spend their time between London and Cornwall. Pete has worked in the surf shop for the past two summers trying to earn a bit of extra money to put towards his year out when he plans to go backpacking around Australia. My heart pangs at the thought of him going away for a year. His parents run a Bed & Breakfast in Bude. Pete hates staying there, having to make polite conversation with a load of strangers. If he hangs around for too long his mum makes him help out. When he's working during the week, he stays with his mate in a bedsit and sleeps on his surf board. How cool is that. I listen intently to everything Pete says. I am completely drinking him up. He is the coolest, sexiest man alive and he's here with me. Pete is seventeen and is in the last year of his A levels. He's going to take a year out when he's finished before he goes to uni. I so want to go with him. I will have finished my GCSE's by the time he sets off. I could delay my A levels for a year; like my mum would ever agree to that!

I tell Pete about my wish to work in television. I am a little vague about the detail but explain that I just want to be involved in the whole thing from moving it from paper onto the screen. He seems really interested in everything I tell him.

As the night draws on, we talk about all kinds of stuff. He tells me about where he has surfed and some of the scary experiences he has had. When I ask him the height of the highest wave he has ever rode, he tells me that waves are not measured in feet and inches but in increments of fear. How cool is that? He goes on to say that the highest wave he ever rode almost made him shit his pants, so I am guessing it was pretty high.

When the bell for last orders rings, I want to shout stop. I don't want this night to end, not ever. Pete has a lift picking him up at twelve thirty. I look across at my mum to see where she is at; is she looking to leave or is she, too, defying the bell? Thankfully, she is defying the bell. However, minutes afterwards she wanders over.

"Jessica, love" she slurs, "we are going to go back to Jean's for a bit, you know, it being our last night. Here, take the key to the caravan. Trevor has the other, we will see you back there in a bit. We will be back no later than twelve thirty." I'm speechless. Really? I'm nodding and smiling and then she stops.

"Who's this?" she says looking at Pete.

"This is Pete, Mum."

"Hello, Pete," she says. How old are you?"

"Seventeen," he responds."

"She's fifteen so don't get any ideas."

"Yes, ma'am," says Pete. I want the ground to swallow me up.

"No funny business, Jessica. You hear?"

"Yes, Mum," I say, cringing. Just piss off already will you, I think. After a momentary glance at us both, she gives a small smile and wanders back over to her crowd. Five minutes later, they all leave the club. Jayne and Simon have by now returned from their little walk around the park. I hadn't even noticed they had gone.

"Where's your mum?" asks Jayne.

"She's gone back to Jean's until twelve thirty."

"Awesome," says Jayne smiling at Simon. Simon whispers in her ear. "Right, well, Simon and I are going to go back to his caravan for a bit. I'll see you back at the caravan at 12.25, yeah?"

"Yeah," I say.

I'm holding the caravan key, winding it through my fingers. "So, fancy, er, coming back to mine for a bit, you know to hang out?" I ask, feeling really nervous now. Pete puts his hand on my knee.

"I'd love to." We stand up. I walk out of the club first and then feel his hand slip into mine. My heart skips a bit. I daren't look at him as he will see I am beaming from ear to ear.

When we get to the caravan, I fuss about offering him something to drink. I offer him a beer but he declines. Instead, I pour two glasses of Dandelion and Burdock. Pete goes to sit on the settee. I fuss some more pulling the curtains closed, never trusting the visibility of net curtains when the lights are on. I sit down close to Pete but not too close. I am so fucking giddy. This is it; I'm going to go to third base tonight. Just wait until Jayne hears. I am so excited. Not only am I going to third base but I'm going there with someone I really care about, not just someone I picked up off the street to try catch up with Jayne. He shuffles closer on the settee.

"Jess, can I kiss you?" he asks. I can't speak. It feels like my lips are welded shut so I nod. He places his lips on mine and somehow, I manage to break them apart and we kiss. His lips are really soft and salty tasting. As we continue to kiss, the intensity deepens. He puts his hand around the back of my neck drawing me even closer to him. I feel his hand move around from the back of my neck down my back. I don't know where to put my hands. I visual myself as Charlene kissing Jason on Neighbours. What would Charlene do? I reach my hand up and place it on his cheek. His hand moves from my back across my arm and onto my left boob. I inhale slightly but don't stop him. It actually feels really nice. Second base – get in! His other hand than moves for the other boob. I like it. I can feel my nipples stick out. I move my hand from his face and move it down his back. One of his hands then starts to move down from my boob and rests on the zip of my shorts. He starts to gently apply pressure. I'm a little taken by surprise and almost choke on the salvia that's building inside my mouth.

"Is it too much?" he asks as he pulls away.

"No," I say. "I want to… I just, I… it felt nice," I say. Nice is a gross understatement. It felt amazing. As soon as his hand went there my whole body started tingling. I had the most amazing sensation in my bits. They were hungry for his touch and still are. I can feel a dampness between my legs. Pete leans in and kisses me again, this time he has one hand at the back of my neck and the other is undoing my zip. I help him ease down my shorts. He then places his hand inside my knickers and I cannot help but let out a huge groan. He kisses me harder now and then I feel his finger inside me. Oh, my God, this feels amazing. He thrusts his finger inside my vagina, up and down. I can hardly kiss him back, I am gasping. I try to focus and begin to wonder whether or not I shouldn't be doing something to him right now. That's the polite thing to do, right? I reach my hand down and place it on his groin. I can feel his erection in his shorts. Without hesitation, he moves his other hand and unzips his shorts. I place my hand inside and place it on top of his boxer shorts. His penis feels really hard. Without realising, my hand is suddenly through the gap at the front of his boxer shorts and is touching his penis. It's his time to gasp. He places his hand over mine and demonstrates how I should hold it. I start to move my hand up and down his penis. It's not as gross as I imagined, there is actually something quite erotic about it. He pauses for a minute from fingering me and appears to enjoy what I am doing to him. Once the initial shock of holding his penis passes by, I begin to get comfortable and take a tighter grasp, realising the tighter I squeeze, the louder he groans. I start moving my hand up and down a little faster. This seems to be sending him into a kind of frenzy. He starts kissing me all over my neck and then I feel two of his fingers inside me. My body responds well to this, despite feeling a little stretched and the tingling sensation reappears. It feels like it's building. It's becoming stronger and stronger. I want it, I need it, I feel the pressure building. I'm going to explode. Suddenly I let out an almighty groan. Fucking hell, my snatch is throbbing. I am free, released from the pressure that's been building inside of me. It feels amazing, euphoric. I'm panting slightly. I guess this is what Jayne means by an orgasm. No wonder she's always at it with someone… anyone. I can see how it can be addictive. I then realise that Pete's penis no longer feels as hard and that my hand feels sticky. So, this is what coming is. It's all making sense, finally.

"I'm sorry," he says.

"For what?" I ask, "That was amazing," I say. I must be beaming again. I feel positively happy. Just then the door barges open. Crap. Pete and I race to pull up our pants and shorts.

"Don't worry, it's only me," shouts Jayne. Oh, thank goodness for that. "Ooh, looks like you two have been having fun." At this, Simon sticks his head around the caravan door, watching us fasten our shorts.

"It's twenty-five past, Jess," says Jayne. Despite her outburst, I am pleased she has reminded me of the time. Simon then says he can hear someone. He kisses Jayne and disappears from the caravan. Jayne disappears into the bathroom. Oh no, this is it, I'm leaving tomorrow and we haven't even discussed how we are going to keep in touch. I can hear my mother.

"You better go," I say. He makes his way out of the caravan.

"Jess, how can I get in touch with you?"

"I can hear her, wait over there," I say, pointing towards the bins. "Give me five minutes." Pete legs it behind the caravan, just as my mother and Trevor come into view. My mum is sobbing.

"I'm just going to miss them sooo much. Hi, Jess," slurs my mother as she walks into the caravan. She goes straight into her bedroom. Trevor eyes me suspiciously. He notices the two glasses of untouched dandelion and burdock, probably thinking how odd it is that Jayne and I poured these and then didn't drink them.

"Where's Jayne?" he asks, but just then Jayne emerges from the bathroom, having showered. Odd I think. Why would she have showered but then it hits me. I quickly check Trevor to see if he has twigged. He looks from me to Jayne and says nothing.

"I'll go check on your mother. You girls get to bed," he says. I nod. I wait until he has gone into their room. My mother is flat out on the bed snoring. I go into our bedroom and sit and wait. I can hear Trevor in the bathroom. I wait until he has finished. The minute I hear one door open and another close I know it's safe.

"Cover for me, Jayne," I whisper as I quietly open the caravan window.

"What are you doing, Jess?"

"Just cover for me, OK," and with that I am outside. I can see Pete stood by the bins. I run up to him. He is smiling. I am in his arms and he is kissing me.

"Here," I say. "Here is my number, call me." He takes the paper and puts it in his shorts pocket.

"I'll call you tomorrow night," he says. "Did you bring a pen?" he asks.

"I didn't," I say. Crap. I debate going back into the caravan.

"Don't worry," he says. "I will ring you tomorrow and then you can take my number." I smile.

I then hear a, "Jess, what are you doing?" Bugger.

"Nothing," I hear Jayne say back, trying to mimic me.

"I better go," I say. We kiss and I feel the same warm sensation all over my body. He watches me climb back into the caravan through the window and I watch him walk off out of distance.

"Tonight has been the best night ever," I say to Jayne.

"It sure has," she replies.

"The perfect end to the holiday," I reply, but Jayne is already snoring.

The following morning, we leave the caravan park slightly later than planned. My mother has to try and cure herself of her hangover first and then there is another tearful goodbye to Jean. No one speaks as we start on the way home. Jayne and I have our Walkman's on and with the words of Chicago blasting in my ears and a smile on my face, hours have passed, *"If you leave me now, you take away the biggest part of me…"* I can tell my mother is asleep in the front because there is no chatter. All I can think about is Pete. I daydream about us both backpacking around Australia.

By the time we reach Nottingham my mother has surfaced and pipes up, "Well, hopefully BT will have sorted out our phone when we get home. The new number should have been posted out so no more nuisance calls. I'm sick of the bloody phone ringing three times and hanging up," she says to Trevor.

"What?" I practically scream. "What do you mean, new number?"

"I've changed the phone number, love. Don't worry, it will still work, just with a new number."

"Oh my God, why would you do that?"

"Calm down, love. You can give it to your friends, they can still call you."

"But the old number… what's happened to that?"

"Well, it's gone… is no more, hasta la vista, Old Number!"

"Yeah, yeah, I get it," I reply. I'm speechless. I can see Trevor is looking at me through his rear-view mirror. I can't believe it. Pete will think I deliberately gave him the wrong number. How can this be happening? My true love cannot contact me. I fight to keep back the tears. Jayne reaches out and grabs my hand and looks truly sorry for me. No more Pete. I can't even contact him through the shop as it was his last shift for the summer today. I know I am never going to see him again and I am crying now, quietly, I just can't help it. I cry all the way back to Ossett. Trevor never looks back again. When we get home, I run upstairs, slam my door and throw myself on my bed. The sobbing continues, I'm not sure if it will ever stop.

Part Two

Chapter Eight
April 1991

This is it. Tonight is the night. Alec and I have been going out for three months now. We have gone through every base and then back over them again and are ready for the next move, sex. Alec's parents are away for the night. My mum thinks I'm at a sleepover at my friend Alice's house. Alice knows all about the night. She's going out with Alec's best friend, Tom. They are going to have sex next Saturday when his parents are out, and I am covering for Alice. I spend quite a bit of time with Alice these days. She's in my A level art class. We both giggled when we had to draw a naked man and our friendship blossomed from there. Jayne is a bit jealous, she uses any opportunity she can to slag Alice off but spends so much time with her boyfriend, Aaron, that I don't see that much of her at the minute.

Alec and I have discussed tonight in detail. Perhaps a little too much. The first discussion was of course contraception and whilst I am on the pill to help my periods, I have told him he has to wear a condom. Well, actually, it wasn't quite put like that. I would never be so bold to use the actual words such as sex and condom. Instead we talked about making the bed and to make sure the bed is made properly, we had to make sure it has a protective sheet on the mattress to make sure no nasty's nasties can get through. I have no idea how a bed became a euphemism for sex but somehow it did.

I can tell Alec is nervous when I arrive at his house. He has already spilled his Carlsberg down his t-shirt and burnt the popcorn. He has chosen a video for us to watch from the video shop, *Conan the Barbarian*. I was thinking more along the lines of Grease, but I don't challenge it. He offers me a can of Carlsberg Special Brew, but I decline. I don't want any lager tonight. I need to keep in control, which is actually, the complete opposite of what I need. I should have a lager to help me relax, I realise that much later.

Alec has done it once already with some French girl he met in Eurocamp last summer. It doesn't bother me. He knows I had already gone to third base, I am just waiting on the home run. He doesn't know I have had an orgasm (administered by someone other than myself). He started asking me questions once about my third base experience, but I told him I don't like talking about it. I like Alec. He's quite funny. I never thought I would go for a ginger so was surprised when I said yes when he asked me out, but I enjoy his company. He's two years older than me and is at Sheffield University studying architecture. He comes home each weekend. We met when I was out in Ossett with Jayne, underage drinking. He had been giving me the eye all night. When a fight broke out in the Manhattan pub, he came over and deliberately moved me out of harm's way. I liked that, so I agreed to go out on a date with him.

We watch the film, barely speaking other than to press pause whilst I go for a wee. When the film finishes, it's ten thirty. We decide to watch Clive Anderson's *Talks Back*. Hardly the stuff to get you in the mood. At eleven thirty, we go up to bed. This is announced by Alec, who blurts out, "Shall we go to bed now?" I agree and carry out the same bedtime routine I do at home. Take my make-up off, cleanse, tone, moisturise, brush my teeth, have a wee and slip on my nightie. I keep my knickers and bra on underneath. I'm not going to make this too easy for him. As I lie in Alec's single bed, I begin to wonder if this is what everyone does before they have sex. Alec puts on his Hi-Fi and presses play to *Darling Nikki* by Prince. *"I knew a girl named Nikki and I guess you could say she was a sex fiend...,"* sings Prince. Hardly. I hardly feel like a sex fiend right now.

Alec strips off, leaving just his boxer shorts on. He lays next to me in bed and asks if I want the light on or off. "Off," I say. I don't want him to see my face. We start kissing and within minutes, he's already pulled off my knickers. He fingers me for a little way but it's more like he's sticking his dib dab into his sherbet. I am not sure if he's just nervous or actually really doesn't know what he is doing. The last time he fingered me I was pretty drunk so don't really remember it. He's trying to warm me up, but it isn't happening. This doesn't seem to bother Alec. He's like a kid in a candy store. A few minutes after prodding the inside of my snatch, I can hear the rustling of a packet and he's sticking on the condom. He then lays on top of me.

"I'm going to put it in now," he announces. It's all a bit official. It's not this official when the nurse pops the speculum inside me for a smear test. I feel Alec dabbing his cock around my vagina. Since he is aiming for the taint (bit between the vagina and anus, I learnt that in sex ed), I guide him to the correct place. He tries thrusting his knob inside but it's a little dry. I lick my finger and moisten the area to help him along. Eventually, he is inside me. It's not how I thought it would feel. Alec seems to be having some sort of fit. He is jerking about on top of me. I feel no pleasure. It hurts actually and after what must only be about two minutes, although it seems a lot longer, I ask him to stop. He turns on the light.

"Did you not like it?" he asks, turning the light on and looking really concerned.

"It was fine," I lie. "I guess it being my first time, it just hurt a bit that's all. Can we try again another time?"

"Course, say in ten minutes or something?" he asks.

"I was thinking another day actually."

"Oh," says Alec. He looks put out now. He sits there looking at his knob. I know what I should do but I just can't face giving him a wank now. My bits feel really sore and I am suddenly really tired. I leave him sat there contemplating what to do with his knob.

"I think I'll go for a shower."

"That's a good idea," I reply. I lay there for five minutes, thinking that perhaps I should have had a few drinks then maybe I would have been more relaxed and it wouldn't have hurt so much. I'm disappointed that my first time was so disappointing. Of course, I will never tell Alec that. I don't hear him come back into the room. I must have fallen asleep. I wake up the next morning to Alec stomping about his bedroom. He's in a mood. I can tell as he always looks more ginger when he's in a mood.

"My parents will be back soon so…" So I need to go, is the message I am getting. I get out of bed. Holy cow. My snatch is on fire. It feels like there is sandpaper rubbing in it as I walk. The only way I can walk is with my legs wide apart. I have a quick shower, hoping the water might take away the stinging, but it doesn't. Alec gives me a quick kiss as I leave and agrees to pick me up at six tonight. We are going ice skating with Alice and Tom. I head to Alice's house which is just around the corner from Alec's. She wants all the sordid detail.

Ten minutes later, I am sat in Alice's room with a cold flannel stuffed between my legs. She says I can keep the flannel, she doesn't want it back. When I describe the events of the previous evening, she looks a little downhearted.

"Don't worry," I assure her. "Yours will go so much better. Make sure you watch something romantic first, like *Pretty Woman*, or Kevin Costner. Now he gives me a proper wide on." We both giggle.

"He's a bit old for you, isn't he," sniggers Alice.

"Even better," I reply. "At least he'll know what he's doing. I'm sure the warm up won't include, *Conan the Barbarian*, popcorn and a tin of special brew!"

"Aww, poor Alec, did he throw you over his back and carry you upstairs in true Conan style?" laughs Alice.

"Hardly, it was more like the announcement for the 10 o'clock news, And now ladies and gentlemen, it's time for sex," I say using my deepest voice. It's at this point, of course, that Alice's mum walks into her bedroom.

"Excuse me," she says, eyeing me suspiciously. Crap! "I just wondered if you girls wanted a sausage sandwich?" Well, at this, we can't contain our laughter. The tears start rolling down my cheek. I'm trying really, really hard not to laugh. Alice is in bits. My whole body is jerking, trying to disguise the laughter.

"Oh, for goodness sake," says Alice's mum. "There are some freshly cooked downstairs if you want some, help yourselves." With that she is gone, and we roll about laughing hysterically. I am holding onto my snatch trying to stop the soreness as I roll.

You would think ice skating would be a good idea when your bits are on fire. Cold air, widened legs but it actually hurts like hell. Every move I make causes me to flinch. Alice and Tom are gliding about the ice arena. Alec tries to skate alongside me, but I can tell he's getting pissed off with how long each glide takes. In the end, he leaves me to it. I resume my position back on the bench and watch the others skate. Why don't they warn you about this in sex ed? I'm sure it would put a lot off the idea.

Alec decides not to come home from uni the weekend after. He calls me to say he has too much work on. Then the following Friday I get a letter dumping me. Something about going to have to stay over at uni more and it will it harder for us to be together. Yeah, right. We are talking Sheffield not bloody London. I'm surprised at myself that I am actually upset. I liked Alec, but I wouldn't call it love, so I don't really understand why I'm upset. I write him a shitty letter back because it makes me feel better. As I am writing, it then dawns on me why I'm so upset; Alec dumping me means of course we won't be hanging out as a four any more. Since Alice likes to spend almost every living minute with Tom, it means I will see less of her (FYI, she actually goes on to marry him and they have four kids). I think it's this that makes me weep but I write back anyway:

~~Dear~~ Alec,

Thanks for your letter. You beat me to it. I realised after that night at yours just how little we have in common. For a start, I'm an Aries and you are Cancer. I don't enjoy your choice of VHS's nor am I particularly keen on Prince. I think the problem is, you are just too steady for me. I like a bit of fire and not in a ginger way I've decided.

It was good of you to write to end it. Of course, a real man would have said it to my face, like I would have done to you, but whatever.

See you around or not.

Jessica

*P.S I looked up the word 'pleasure' in the Oxford dictionary, meaning **'a feeling of happy satisfaction and enjoyment'** – something you should work on.*

I wipe the last tear away. Perhaps I just don't like being dumped, or maybe being single. Pah. I need a man, not a boy, I decide. I open my Just17 Magazine and rip out the double page photo of Kevin Costner to stick on my wall. He can keep me company for a while.

Chapter Nine
Christmas 1991

Jayne and I are stood in her garage wearing matching red and black crushed velvet dresses she secretly ordered from Kays catalogue. It's snowing outside and it feels like a proper Christmas. We are sipping her grandad's home-made wine which she has nicked out of her mum's sideboard. It tastes like potatoes on its own but mix it with lemonade and it's not too bad. Both Jayne and I are single right now which seems to have helped us reconnect our friendship somewhat. There has been no one else since Alec (I decided to take a break from boys/men for a while. OK, so maybe no one has come along). Jayne and Aaron are on another of their many breaks, although Jayne says it's official this time. I don't really care, it's just nice to have my best friend back for a while.

We are buzzing about the garage. We plan out our pub route tonight. First, it will be the Harpenters Arms, then over the road to the Duck 'n' Bottle. Next, the Horse and Cart followed by the Tavern and ending up in the Manhattan Bar to end Christmas Eve. Tonight, we are on a snogathon. We are going to see how many Christmas snogs we can get in one night. Jayne has purchased fresh mistletoe from Ossett market, mine is placed delicately under my flashing Christmas tree head band, whilst Jayne has hers attached her to her halo.

After downing the rest of Grandad's home-made wine, we sneak out of her garage and make our way into Ossett. We walk down the snicket of death, as we like to call it. It's so narrow and dark and completely freaks me out every time I go down there, day or night. With the snow, it lights up quite nicely, but we decide to leg it, running as fast as we can in the snow. It's not scary tonight. Nothing is scary. Tonight is exciting. It's my first pub crawl at Christmas in Ossett. Friday nights are always lively ones but tonight will be exceptional, I just know it.

As we run of out the bottom of the snicket, we find ourselves bumping into two police officers. Oh crap. I am still underage, and getting busted at this stage in the evening is not going to make a great night.

"Everything all right, girls?" asks Officer number one.

"Fine," we reply in unison.

"Where you off to?" asks Officer number two. It's by this point I notice that Officer one and Officer two are really quite hot.

"Just up town," replies Jayne, making fuck me eyes at Officer number one. He doesn't seem interested.

"Here," says Officer number two. "You dropped your mistletoe." He picks it up and hands it over to me, reaching slightly above my head.

"Well, if you insist," he says, leaning in with his lips pouted. Whoa. I've pulled a policeman. I give him a smacker on the lips. "Have a good night, girls," says Officer number two. Check me out, I say to myself. Just down the snicket and catch myself a bobby. I look at Jayne to see if she is as excited as I am right now. That'll be a no. She looks pissed off. Probably a bit strange that someone rejected her fuck me eyes. Oh well, there are plenty more just waiting for us. I link through Jayne's arm and we march our way into Ossett town centre.

As expected, the place is heaving. The pubs are full which is a good thing as it gives the bar staff less time to wonder whether or not I am underage. As we fight our way to the bar, I notice there is a kerfuffle going on in the corner of the bar. People are cheering, probably another pleb has just downed a pint whilst standing on their head, I think to myself. We get our half lagers and black after chuntering that they charge an extra five pence for the black, sixty pence for half a lager really is now taking the piss, especially when I only get three pounds pocket money a week.

We find a space in the corner of the pub with a shelf for us to put our drinks on. Jayne is looking around, eyeing up her prey. I stand there, very aware that the new G-string knickers I bought from Knickerbox earlier today are not just G-string in my butt but G-string in my snatch. It's very uncomfortable. I wriggle slightly from side to side, trying to keep in with the beat of the music from the juke box. I can sense Jayne is on edge. No one is paying us any attention. She needs to trump my police officer kiss which to be fair, will take some trumping. I get a little concerned when I notice she is eyeing the fire alarm. Pulling a fireman would be a good trump to a police officer I guess.

"Let's play a drinking game," she pipes up. I wonder whether my six pounds budget for tonight can withhold a drinking game but then, if tonight goes like other nights we have been on, I usually have had several drinks bought for me and enough change for a bag of chips and scraps on the way home.

"Fuzzy Duck," starts Jayne.

"Fuzzy duck," I reply.

"Fuzzy duck," says Jayne a little louder this time, oh, and we have a bite.

"Fuzzy duck," says some random male who looks old enough to be my dad.

"Fuzzy duck," replies Jayne, now smiling from ear to ear.

Another male joins in, "Ducky fuzz," he says, switching the words.

I reply, "Fuck he does." Bollocks. I drink two fingers full of my half. The game continues. By the time we are finished, our close twosome has grown to a large eightsome. We are no longer drinking halves but have pints and my duck is completely fucked. We stagger out of the Harpenters with our new pals. OK, so they may be slightly older but that has its advantages, I have £5.40 in my purse still.

We wander over to the Duck 'n' Bottle and within a few minutes I am handed a bottle of Castaway. I feel my stomach flip. This is our first reunion since the Cricket Club. Thankfully, there is no Diamond White to compliment it so it's drinkable. However, I am reminded of the fruity taste at the back of my throat as it goes down, remembering the same fruity taste as it was coming back up. Having secured our drinks, Jayne and I wander a little further from the packed bar. Jayne now seems happy to take a side step from her new friends. As we head near the pool table, I notice my friend, Clark, is playing pool.

"Hey, Clark, Merry Christmas," I say.

"Oh, and a Merry Christmas to you as well, Jessica." Clark is really posh, like proper posh. He goes to the private school in Batley. His folks moved up here from London a couple of years ago. His dad is one of those lawyers that wears a wig. I met Clark on a night out. I found him searching the floor for his glasses. I thought he was pissed but then I realised that somebody had swiped them off him and thrown them to where he couldn't see them. I thought all that kind of shit was over when you left school but clearly not. I'd helped him find them and since then we became friends who chatted when I was out in Ossett. He once bought me a Taboo and lemonade which is expensive stuff. I think it was his way of saying thank you.

As I chat to Clark, Jayne is resting on the side of the pool table. When Clark tries to take his shot, Jayne lifts her drink and raises her arse cheek to assist him with the move. I can tell it's not the angle Clark needs, but he is too posh and polite to say anything. It's at this point one of the burly looking guys we have been playing fuzzy duck with, comes over. He's not looking too friendly.

"You're a right cock," he says to Clark.

"Yes, I'm very well thank you, are you all right, cock?" Clark replies, looking slightly euphoric, thinking he had finally been accepted amongst the Yorkshire folk. Maybe the slap on the shoulder was too much, for the next thing I see, Clark is on the floor with a blooded nose. Bless him, he hasn't yet mastered the Yorkshire lingo. After seeing Clark up, I can't help but lose it with the buffoon.

"Here," I say, handing back the Castaway of which I have had one sip. "Stick that up your arse, it'll help you locate your brain." Jayne pops off the pool table. She is glaring at me but I don't care. After checking Clark is OK, I tell Jayne with some authority, "We are off." I drag her outside. She is miffed.

"What did you do that for?" she asks. "They would have paid for our whole night out."

"That was Clark, he hit, my friend. I don't care what he paid for, I'm not having any of that shit," I reply. I'm quite surprised at myself for standing up to Jayne. A few months ago, I wouldn't have dared disagree with her about anything in case she no longer wanted to be my mate but now, well, I have principles and that tosser crossed a line.

"So where next then?" she asks with a hint of sarcasm. "The Tavern will be dead now, no one will arrive for at least another hour." I think.

"Well, I guess we will get good seats for a change," I find myself saying. I start walking off in the direction of the Tavern. I can sense she is still stood on the spot but I keep walking. I promise myself that once I get past the florists I will turn around to make sure she is following me but there is no need, she's at my side.

"Crikey Jess, you pop your cherry and look at you go. The gloves are off..." I giggle a little. Jayne giggles a little. I think she has forgiven me.

She is right, of course. We arrive in the Tavern Pub and there is barely anyone there other than the heavy metal freaks who sit almost on the DJ station listening to Metallica and Iron Maiden. This is one of those pubs where it hasn't quite defined itself as a pub or a club. There is a DJ station which plays mainly rock music, there is a dance floor which your feet literally stick to, it has a beer garden where if you fall off your chair, you will definitely need a tetanus jab and a really large car park where all the boy racers rev their engines. It's a weird place but somehow, it has an appeal to it. Jayne and I order another two lager and blacks and dare to sit on the stools, the furthest away from the DJ station as possible. We sip our drinks and wait for everyone else to arrive. After another four half lager and blacks we are beginning to get seriously bored. Where is everyone? People should have been arriving at least forty-five minutes ago. I can tell the bar staff are thinking the same thing as more staff has arrived. The lady who mops up the sick from the toilets has arrived and even she is looking perplexed. Jayne is freaking out. She won't sit still. "Let's go outside," she says.

We grab our drinks and head outside. There is thick snow everywhere and not a soul in sight. Jayne makes us sit on a picnic bench. Some people walk past the pub, we can hear them, "Can you believe it, Hawks Span are in Ossett." Jayne and I stare at one another.

"Oi," shouts Jayne. She runs out of the beer garden and onto the path outside. "What do you mean, Hawks Span are in Ossett?"

"Ain't you heard?' says the male. Jayne is giving a look that suggests, of course I haven't fucking heard or why else would I be talking to you! "Their coach broke down on the way back from Leeds, the taxis aren't going far because of the snow so they are stuck in Ossett for the night. Word has it, they are playing in Woburn House." Fuck me. Jayne and I are marching towards Woburn House. As we arrive, I can see a massive queue has formed all the way down the street.

"Ah fuck," shouts Jayne. "We've no chance."

"Just a minute," I say. I walk up to the bouncer outside the front of the entrance. I can see all those queuing looking at me like they are about to glass me any minute. The bouncer is glaring at me. I don't recognise him. He must be new.

"Is Gerard here?" I ask. The bouncer looks at me.

"Who are you?" he asks.

"A close friend," I respond. He doesn't look happy, but I keep my feet firmly in place. He whispers something in his microphone. I wait. We wait. Jayne impatiently waits, pissed off watching more people join the queue.

Five freezing minutes later, Gerard arrives. "Jess," he announces, hugging me. Jayne's jaw drops. "How you been sweetheart, I've missed you?"

"All good, thanks. You know, bit of this, bit of that."

"Want to come in?" he asks.

"Can we?" I say.

"Just the two of you?"

"Yeah, just us."

"We're so busy. Hawks Span are here, they are going to do a set later." Gerard walks through with us into the bar area. "Right hun, I've got to split. Great to see you, don't be a stranger." Gerard kisses my cheek and disappears into the crowd. Jayne is staring at me now like she doesn't know me.

"How the hell...?" she starts.

"It used to be a gym, don't you remember? Gerard owns the building and used to be in here every second of the day." She's still staring. "You know, when my arse expanded to the size of Ireland, I joined the gym, went religiously for about six months, we became cross training buddies, although he only did about five minutes and then went on the sunbed." Jayne looks flabbergasted. I can tell she is wondering how I have done all of these things under her radar but the truth is, she's been so fixated on Aaron, I've had to become independent of her. I can tell she doesn't like it, but we are in here and for that I know she is grateful. Hawks Span aren't playing yet so we need to head to the bar.

"I need a wizz," says Jayne. That's her code for my money is running is out so I am going to pretend to go to the toilet so you can get the drinks in and, the sucker that I am, lets it ride. I head to the bar. It's packed.

"Jess," I hear being shouted. I turn to look. Gerard is pointing to a door with a huge burly bouncer stood outside. Go in there, you'll get served quicker. Thankfully, the burly-looking bouncer hears and sees Gerard so when I walk over to the door, I am let through without any to-do. I walk into the room. It's busy, but not as busy as the bar outside. I wait for my place in line until I am finally at the front of the bar. As I order my drinks, I turn to the left and there he is, the lead singer of Hawks Span, Mickey Vain. There is a huge part of me that just wants to jump up and down and scream right now but I know if I do that, my feet won't touch the ground and I will probably be slung out onto the snowy street. No, I have to play it cool. I look across, he looks at me, I give a slight smile and turn to the bartender. I battle with myself to not look to my right. It's hard, every inch of my body is telling me to look right. Oh jeez, I can't resist. I look right. He is staring. I turn to my left to see if he is looking at the person to the left of me but it's a bloke. I know Mickey Vain is definitely heterosexual. There are always photos of him in the *Daily Mirror* with some young girl. I see he is looking at me but this time he cocks his head slightly to the side, a look of questioning crosses his face. I wonder what this might mean. Do I have something on my face? Not another bloody blackcurrant ring around my lips from my half lagers and black, please no. The bartender is a distraction. I choose not to order two half lagers and black but instead decide to order something more sophisticated.

"Two taboo and lemonades," I request.

"That'll be £3.00," the bartender replies. Shit, that's my money gone and no change for a bag of chips and scraps. I start to hand over my money until a hand is covering my hand.

"Allow me," says Mickey Vain. He pulls my hand back towards me and nods at the bar man. "Make them a double," he says. My knees are knocking. The closest I have ever been to a celebrity was at the Wakefield Theatre when Rodney and Emu came on tour and I got my picture taken with them. Somehow this feels a lot different.

"Thanks," I manage. I can feel my bottom lip is quivering with excitement.

He chinks my glass. "Cheers."

"Cheers," I manage back.

"So, tell me, what's a pretty little thing like you doing in a shit hole like this?"

"Aw, I bet you say that to all the girls," I reply.

"I really don't," he says, "I usually see them back stage or at my hotel room," he winks.

"Hey, it's not that bad. We have our own football team, a town hall, a great market and we are pretty skilled in the old cloth making business."

"Wow, that's bitchin," he replies.

"Well go on then," I say. "Where are you from?"

"London, baby," he says. OK, I can't compete there. As I take a sip of my drink, someone comes over and whispers in Mickey's ear. Shit. Were they telling him I am under age. Crap.

"Gotta jam. You sticking around?" he asks. Oh yes, like a magnet to his zip. I nod. It's all I can do. He downs his drink. I down mine as well. I'm not really sure why but it seems like the right thing to do. He walks out the side door at the other side of the bar. I sit there, gobsmacked. Did that really just happen. I am smiling.

"I think you pulled there, love," says the bartender. It's like he is reading my mind. I'm glad he thinks I pulled too. It's good to have a second opinion. I was wondering whether that was a definite pull or just a bored chit chat before he goes on stage. Since the bartender was present throughout, I decide it was a definite pull.

I leave the small invitation only bar area, something I later discover is called the 'VIP lounge', and go to find Jayne. I see her wandering around continuing to look totally pissed off. I walk up to her with the one drink in my hand, having downed mine at the bar.

Before I can say anything, "Aw cheers, mate, thanks for the drink she says," grabbing the taboo out of my hand, knocking it back. That was my Mickey Vain drink. I was planning on taking that home and placing it in some kind of glass cage.

"You'll never guess who I have just seen," she says.

"Er, Mic…"

"Aaron. And he's here with that cheap tart from Lupset."

"Oh, well, I just met Mick…"

"If he thinks I'm getting back with him, he can think again. Come on, let's go over here and where were you? I was looking everywhere." She asks the question but isn't interested in the answer. We leave the bar area and head into the main room where the stage is. The DJ is still playing. The curtains on the stage are still drawn but I can hear an electric guitar being tuned. My heart starts beating to the rhythm.

Jayne insists we move as close towards the stage as possible. Apparently, it has nothing to do with the fact Aaron and his bit are sat on the seats near the front but that's fine by me. We get as close as humanly possible. Jayne starts swaying her hips to the beat of MC Hammer, *U Can't Touch This*. I try to dance but it's quite awkward when you don't like the music. I decide to head back to the bar. Having been spared the cost of the taboo drinks, I can afford us another couple of rounds of lager and black. By the time I get back, Jayne is smooching with Aaron to Wonder Stuff's, *The Size of a Cow*. Not really a smoochie track but they are giving it a good shot. I can see the Lupset tart sat in the corner, firing venom out of her mouth. I quickly turn away for fear of making eye contact which means I am likely to be glassed. Just then, a loud strum of an electric guitar plays. The DJ music quietens and the curtains start to pull back. There is an almighty cheer around the building and within seconds, everyone has congregated into the main hall. Mickey's head is down over the microphone, as the electric guitar plays, his body trembles to each strum of the note. God, he's sexy. His whitewash tight denim trousers show every inch of his muscular legs and the pouch at the top looks like it hides a whole army. Tucked into his jeans is a plain black vest that clings to his torso. His tanned, tattooed, muscular arms are exposed and they are grasping the microphone. As he lifts his head, his eyes are closed. He delicately moves the strand of jet-black, shoulder-length hair from his face and parts his lips. He is getting ready. I am ready, in fact, I am so fucking ready I am bouncing about like Bambi on steroids. When he starts to sing, that is it. I have lost all sensation in my body. I have no idea what I am doing. I am mesmerised. It's like I am sailing on a ship and my body is responding to each movement over the turbulent waves.

As the volume builds, the atmosphere in Woburn House is electric. It seems everyone is feeling the same sensations. However, when Mickey sings, "Came so close to a fallen angel, I had to look twice and grabbed it tight…" I swear he is singing these words to me. It's just like my Matt Goss dream, only better. Just as I am searching for confirmation, he rips off his vest and flings it at me. I hold out my arms but some fat bitch dives on it and starts kissing it. Oh well, I don't care. He bought me a taboo and is singing to me.

When they eventually finish their set after three encores, the curtains draw and the DJ kicks off with Deee-Lite's, *Groove is in the Heart*. I stand there, feeling lost. Everyone else seems to have accepted their departure but I am in some kind of trance. I don't know what to do. Even Jayne has pulled herself away from Aaron for three seconds to ask if I am OK. I don't know if I am OK. I feel like I'm on some kind of drug and the only way to stop the effect is for something else euphoric to happen. The problem is, I'm not sure what can now happen. That's probably the last I will ever see of Mickey Vain. Just as that thought starts to sink in I am tapped on the shoulder. I turn to look and stood in front of me is the burly looking bouncer who was guarding the door to the secret bar.

"You are required in the VIP lounge." Holy shit. This is it. I have to pinch myself. Can this really be happening, although it could just be Gerard. I tell Jayne I am off for a bit. We agree to meet outside the club at closing. She doesn't care. Her tongue is down Aaron's throat. I follow the bouncer towards the 'VIP lounge'. I'm a little nervous but still buzzing from the euphoric bubble Hawks Span have put me in.

When I enter the bar, Mickey is nowhere to be seen. I recognise a couple of members from the band and then Gerard comes over to me.

"Jess, wasn't that amazing. Can you believe Hawks Span played here? This will put us on the map." I smile at Gerard. This is a huge success for him and I am genuinely happy for him. I had heard the club was struggling; it had a bad reputation for drugs and had been closed on a number of occasions following police raids. I was kinda of hoping I was called in here for another reason. However, just then the clapping starts and people are on their feet. Mickey Vain walks into the room. He has on a new black vest. He gives a slight nod to the onlookers but heads his way towards Gerard and me.

"Oh, lord, Mickey. I mean, that was just a total knock out man." I stare at Gerard. Somehow those words don't sound quite right coming out of his mouth. He has tried to drop the campness and become more manly. Mickey just nods.

"Taboo?" he says to me.

"No, it was brilliant, I loved it. Who's complaining?" I ask.

"Drink," he says.

"Oh, Taboo, er, yes please," I reply, feeling stupid. Mickey orders himself a bourbon and coke and hands me what looks like a triple Taboo. I just pray he doesn't want me to repeat the round.

"Come," he says, guiding me away from Gerard and into a corner of the bar. I follow like a loyal puppy. I can see people are staring, girls in particular. As we sit down, a couple of girls come over to us.

"Hi, Mickey. Stacey and I were wondering if we could have your autograph," one of them says.

"No, fuck off," he replies. I laugh with shock, watching as they skulk off.

"Wow, that's a bit rude. Aren't they your fans?" I ask.

"What's rude is interrupting me when I am here with you." Oh boy, I like this. I feel the bubble I am in has just expanded another ten inches. I sit there, not knowing what to say. I hate that I am so lacking in the 'talk to a massive rock legend, who's singled you out' department. Why aren't I prepared for this? I've dreamt about scenarios like this for months. OK, maybe not with Mickey, but it's all the same really. Mickey places his hand on the inside of my thigh. It's a bit forward but I like it.

"So," he says, "tell me the naughtiest thing you've ever done." Shit. I think for a bit.

"Erm, well, I once stole some jelly babies from Hillard's. Actually, the cashier didn't scan them, and I didn't realise until I got home later when my mum checked the receipt as she didn't believe the cost of bread, milk, sheer tights and jelly babies came to £3.80." Mickey snorts.

"The dirtiest thing you've ever done, babe." Oh, crap.

For some reason the only thing I can think of is the Desperately Seeking Susan poster. However, I don't want to own up that it only made me feel good, so before I can think, I say, "I masturbated to Desperately Seeking Susan." He's now sucking on my ear lobe. Boy, that feels good. I'm totally out of my comfort zone but decide to go with it.

"How about you?" I ask.

"Babe, I invented the word dirty," he says back, continuing to suck my earlobe. I'm a little put out that he's clearly had a few women in his time but I guess being a rock superstar, that that's inevitable.

"Come on," he says. "Let's get out of here."

"And go where?" I ask, racking my brain as to where might be open at this time of night other than the Bengal Indian House.

"The hotel, babe." My stomach flips. Oh, crapsticks. He wants me to go back to his hotel. This can only mean one thing. SEX. But I'm not very good at the sex thing. My bubble has a leak and common sense is starting to creep in.

"I'm not just one of your groupies who you can fuck and chuck you know. There's more to me than that."

He pulls back and studies me. "Of course, babe. I knew that about you as soon as I saw you in here earlier. You don't know how fed up I am of just hanging out with women who only want me for one thing. It's degrading, man. I've been waiting to meet someone with intellect and gorgeousness (is that even a word?) and then I saw you. Why do you think I insisted on you coming back in here?" Oh, so it was him, not Gerard. Well, that of course, all makes complete sense now. He's not just after a shag but he really, really likes me. I can imagine it does get dreary having women throw themselves at him all the time. No wonder he came looking for me.

"Let's talk," I say. He takes a sip of his drink, rests his head back and starts to tell me how hard it is being on the road all the time. There is never anytime to do anything. Why, he hasn't even managed to get his mum a Christmas present this year. It's not all that it's cracked up to be, it's actually quite lonely. People see it is a glam life, 'Rock n roll,' party upon party but actually it's just the same shit every night. By the time he finishes, my heart is melting for him. This poor guy. All he wants is companionship. Someone to be with. Well funnily enough, that's what I am looking for at the moment.

"Come on, let's go," I say, surprised at myself for being so forward. Perhaps if I hadn't been drinking in his every word, I might have realised that his woe is me story was pretty well rehearsed. Perhaps it has been said a few hundred times. However, hindsight is a wonderful thing and even if I had suspected his tale was not genuine, would it have stopped me from doing what I did next? I don't think so.

Chapter Ten

As soon as we walk into the hotel, I instantly recognise Daniel Sherburn. He was the year above me in school. He's now the night porter at the Fort Hotel in Ossett.

"Evening, Mr Vain," he says, beaming from ear to ear. "Erm, can I get you and Jess, I mean, your guest, anything?"

"Send up some Dom Perignon, nothing older than 1988."

"Yes, sir," replies Daniel. I'm a little impressed he knows my name. Mickey takes my hand and leads me towards the elevator.

"Excuse me, Mr Vain," shouts Daniel, "but won't you be needing your room key?" Mickey stops.

"Fucking useless hotel, still have keys." Daniel hands him the key with a huge wooden fob. I decide not to question how else he would get into his room. Probably he has some kind of electronic door in London that opens when he waves his hand like on *Star Trek*. The fob says 'Chester suite'. Eek. I've been in the hotel before, I had one of my birthday parties here. They do a mean knickerbocker glory but I've never been into one of the rooms. Then again, I was only eight so it would have been a worry if I was in a bedroom, living just down the road and all.

"Just one more thing, Mr Vain," says Daniel. I can tell Mickey is getting frustrated. The vein at the side of his temple is slightly raised. "Would you mind just signing my notebook." Daniel whips out his notepad. Mickey snatches it and the pen and scribbles the words, 'Fuck off'.

"Wow, thanks," says Daniel, delighted Mickey Vain has just written the words 'fuck off' on his notebook. Mickey guides me into the lift. Once in the elevator, he presses floor three because that's the highest number of floors there is. He pushes me against the glass in the elevator and rubs his leg between my thighs. It feels nice, sexy and hot. Before he even has chance to kiss me, the elevator pings and the door opens. He grabs my hand and leads me down the corridor towards the Chester suite.

I'm at the point of no return. Actually, I was at that point when I suggested we leave Woburn House and go to his hotel, but this is the part where the fantasy becomes a reality. He unlocks the door, he gestures me inside. I step inside, he steps inside and the door closes.

Six hours later, I emerge. I am no longer a girl. I am a woman, through and through. The snow has stopped and Daniel gets me a taxi home. I sneak inside the house, praying my mother and Trevor are passed out from the Christmas Eve party they attended. Phew, it's all quiet. I use the downstairs toilet and decide that whilst my teeth probably need brushing more than they have ever needed brushing before, they can wait until the morning, well, later on this morning. I sneak into my bedroom. I get out of my dress and sling it on the bedroom floor. My dress is sullied. I verge between wanting to burn it and wanting to sleep with it.

I can't sleep. I need to write things down to ensure it gets locked in my memory bank and to make sure that some things get repeated in my future – or just in my wank bank. I sit in bed with my pen and notebook. I don't know where to start. How can I describe the last six hours? Heaven with a bit of hell thrown in, maybe? I have so many questions. I decide the only way I can write it down is to write a letter to Sorting Suze. It goes something like this:

Dear Sorting Suze,

I have just had the most amazing experience, ever, I mean ever. I don't think I can ever replicate the last six hours of my life but I need you to answer some questions that are troubling me:

1. Please explain why the sensation of an ice cube mouthed across my nipples sent me into a frenzy and then why I climaxed when it was inserted in my butt.

2. Please, please explain why bending me in so many different positions increased the air in my snatch and why it then blew out with me powerless to stop it? I swear the music to the Land of Hope & Glory trumpeted its way out of my vagina.

3. Why does urinating on a man's head turn him on, even though it was accidental?

4. Sucking toes. What is it about that? It felt good; I kinda wanted it to stop but at the same time I really, really wanted him to suck harder.

5. Can you develop a rash from being internally filled with champagne? Does it make a difference if it's Dom Perignon?

6. Is it normal for a man to want to be tied up and spanked? What's that about? Did he lack a mother's love, and does it matter that I enjoyed it? In fact, I wished I had a whip.

7. Is it normal to have six orgasms in one night? My snatch is throbbing. Is it normal that every time I write the words 'orgasm', 'snatch' and 'throbbing' that I feel like I'm about to have another orgasm?

Yours,

Naughty, fifthly Bunny.

Two weeks later…

When I eventually wake later, it all feels very surreal. Did that just really happen? I reach for the napkin at the side of my bed with the telephone number scribbled on it. It has an obvious digit missing. I laugh. I guess he has handed this number out more times than he has showered in Dom Perignon. However, it still all seems like a dream. I check my left arse cheek and see the huge bite mark. As I lean in, the smell of sex is very present. I ooze it. I like it. I know I will never see Mickey again and I'm OK with this. He gave me the best night of my life so far. There was no romance. Pure filth happened in that hotel room last night and I enjoyed every fucking minute of it. I lie back and close my eyes. If you could see me now, I am smiling from ear to ear. There is then a tapping on my door.

"Jess, Jess, can I come in are you alone?" Of course I am alone, I think to myself. Why wouldn't I be alone? But then I am reminded of those precious previous hours and realise that perhaps I shouldn't be so judgmental of her questioning.

"Come in," I shout, pulling the duvet up to my chin to ensure the smell of sex does not leak out.

"It's twelve thirty, love. You've missed Christmas morning, the pancakes, the Bucks Fizz." Oh.

"Merry Christmas," I manage back.

"Are you coming down, love? Auntie Janet and Uncle Colin will be here soon. You are missing the best bit of the day."

Bloody hell, it's only Christmas Day. It's not like I still believe in Santa Claus. My mother is stood there looking like a wanting puppy. I want to please her, but I also want to lay here and have rude thoughts about the night before. She's still stood there.

"You'll be at uni next year love and who knows what you'll be doing next Christmas; this might be our last together for a while." She has a point. I can't imagine next year I will want to be tossing pancakes and watching my mother get pissed on Bucks Fizz.

"OK, OK, give me ten minutes. I need to, erm, freshen up and then I'll be down." She's smiling now, appeased finally. As she leaves the room, I throw my head back on my pillow. Just imagine, if at age seventeen I can have such amazing sex from just one night, imagine all the orgasms I am going to have in the next four years at uni. I say a silent prayer to the ghost of orgasm past, present and future. I have changed, I want to stay changed. Please, please allow the last twelve hours of my life to be replicated again but this time with the knowledge and the tools to make it even better.

Chapter Eleven
September 1992

This is it. Freedom at last. I stand in the small room that is going to be my home for the next twelve months. OK, so it's smaller than my room at home and looks doubly smaller with my suitcase and boxes in it but the difference between this room and my room at home is, this one has a lock on the door, it has no curfew, it has no demanding mother in the doorway. That door can stay locked for as long as I jolly well want it to. In this place, I am in control of the door and that makes me feel like I am in control of my life! Stood at the door is my mother, sobbing.

"Promise me you will eat properly, promise me you will come home and see me, us. Promise you will be careful, promise you will be safe, I don't know why you couldn't have commuted, Trevor would have picked you up wouldn't you?" she says, nudging Trevor. He nods on demand.

"Mum, we've been through this. It's easier if I just stay in residence this year. I can crack on with my work without the travel from Leeds to Ossett, plus it's a great opportunity to make new friends. You are always going on about how I should extend my friendship circle, especially now Jayne is four months pregnant." She's now doing that thing she does when she's uncomfortable; she is fiddling with her necklace. Her bottom lip is bobbing up and down more times than a dingy crossing the Atlantic.

"Don't worry, Mum," I say, hugging her. "I'll be fine. I'll be home before you know it (already mentally thinking that will be in around eight weeks, unless I am skint and starving), I'll give you a ring when I can." She is still standing there. This is awkward. Thankfully, Trevor steps in.

"Come on, love. Jess has a whole load of things to do so best we be off. Ta-ra love, be careful." Funnily enough, it's those words that hit me and bring out the bobbing dingy at the bottom of my lip. Trevor has never been the emotional one but this time, it's like he really cares and that fills me with something, maybe love? Admiration?

Before I can think any further, I hear the words 'Pot Noodle shots', being shouted down the corridor. I have no idea what that means but it sounds like fun and I want to be a part of it. I hug her again but this time with a slight forceful push, edging her out of my door.

"Call, won't you love?"

"Yes, Mum."

"If you need anything, anything at all, just ring us, anytime, day or night, like three in the morning, four, five, six…" she's shouting as she gets into the lift. I smile, nod, wave and then shut my door behind me, resting my head against it. I look around. OK, so it's not the Ritz but I am so frigging excited. I check the mirror, reapply my very berry lipstick and leave the room, in search of the Pot Noodle shot challenge.

I wander down the hall and follow the sound of cheering. The communal lounge is filled with students, most holding cans of lager in their hands. I can briefly make out two students who look like they are trying to down Pot Noodles as quickly as humanly possible, swallowed down with a mouthful full of Carlsberg. As I begin to wonder why anyone would want to do this, I hear, "bunch of tossers" my sentiments exactly. I turn to see who is reading my mind. Before me is a rug muncher if ever I saw one. Half her head is shaved, she has a piercing in her lip, one in her nose and one in her eyebrow. She is wearing a vest with no bra, tight jeans with chains around her pockets and biker boots. If that doesn't define a rug muncher, I'm not sure what else would. To her side is a tubby, pudding-looking blond who looks like she has been dressed by her grandmother. She seems attached to the rug muncher but not in a "we're a couple" sort of way. I'm intrigued.

"Hi, I'm Jess," I say. Rug muncher looks at me, it's not friendly. Pudding smiles. "I hate Pot Noodles," I add. Nothing. "In fact, I hate the whole charade of let's try to do something totally out there, just to get attention, when clearly all they do usually is play on their playstations." I'm getting somewhere; Rug muncher's eyebrow has raised. I can tell because the earring is now somewhere just underneath her hair line.

"Ha ha. What's a playstation?" Lesbo raises her other eyelid, so much so I think it is tickling the back of her neck.

"Let's just say they are something young boys play with often," I reply, winking at the same time.

"Oh, naughty," she replies. "She's naughty, we're off to the Union Club. Fancy joining us?" asks Pudding.

"Sure," I say, trying not to sound too keen but secretly desperately keen to leave and find myself some friends, any will do right now – even the Addams Family.

Rug muncher turns and walks out of the room without saying a word. Pudding gestures for me to follow so I do. I follow them down the stairs, which is quite bizarre bearing in mind there is a lift and we are on the twelfth floor. Why walk when you don't have to? As if reading my thoughts again, Pudding pipes up, "Charlotte doesn't believe in using short cuts; the long way is the right way." Charlotte stops. I have to say, she doesn't look like a Charlotte, more like a Leigh or a Grace Jones.

"There are many short cuts in life, Alice, I just choose not to take the easy route." Alice, aka Pudding, turns to me and smiles. I smile back.

"So, Jess, oh, I'm Alice by the way, what are you studying?"

"Marketing," I reply. Of course, I was supposed to be doing something to do with television but since I couldn't quite put my finger on what exactly in television, I attempted beauty college after I sat my G.C.S.E.'s, thinking I'd become a make-up artist. I lasted just four weeks; the wax pot scared me off. The school were great and let me start my A levels. Since I wasn't going to be a make-up artist, my careers advisor suggested I do marketing, that way I can sell myself into anything I want and therefore doors will open. It made perfect sense to me, at the time anyway.

"I'm doing my teaching degree, as is Charlotte, er, I mean Charlie." Arr, that's more like it, I think to myself, although still a little taken aback that Rug muncher wants to work with children. She looks like she would eat them as opposed to teach them. I look now at Charlie, who is a few steps ahead. She stops on the step and turns.

"Let's get this straight, I want to teach fifteen to sixteen-year olds philosophy. I figure the only way to change this sorry fucking world is through teaching the next generation." Poetic, I think to myself. I daren't look at Alice for fear she may see the crack in my nodding expression of understanding. Ah, feck it, I do it anyway. Alice is looking at Charlie intently and nodding, but then turns to me once Charlie's back is before us and puts her fake gun fingers to her head and blows. Oh, I like Alice, I think we are going to be mates, although I hope she doesn't mind if I call her Pudding, I've rather taken to that name, Alice somehow doesn't quite fit.

Pudding tells me how she just wants to work with children, any age, she doesn't care, she just loves them. She is the third eldest out of seven children and therefore has some experience in these things. She originates from Middlesbrough, but I'm not judging.

We leave the student digs and Pudding and I follow Charlie into a bar directly opposite named the Union Club. I thought it was some kind of uni bar, nestled in the basement of the student block but it turns out it is actually a pub called the Union Bar. We walk in and it's not what I was expecting. I assumed it would be filled with old gits drowning themselves in pints of Tetley's, playing darts and dribbling on the floor. However, as soon as we walk in, I hear a chorus of "Charlie, we are over here." I look to see if it is the AGM of the rug muncher society, but it turns out to be what looks like the 'in crowd'. Why, there is handsome a lad a plenty along with a good amount of attractive looking females. How come Rug muncher fits in with this crowd? Just then, a tall slim blond stands up. She looks familiar. Turns out she is Rug muncher's twin. She is definitely the twin who got more of the placenta. Why, her hair is so shiny and her eyes are the bluest I have ever seen. It's then I notice that Rug muncher's eyes are blue too, somewhere hidden beneath all that dark black eye liner are two dazzling blue eyes. I'm not sure I am going to fit in with this lot. I'm not sure where exactly I am going to fit in with any of the uni lot. I'm leaning more towards being with the tutors rather than the pupils, having experienced the 'older man', et al. Before I can think up my escape, surprisingly, Charlie is introducing me to the 'in' crowd. I didn't even realise I was really on her radar. Pudding heads to the bar to get us drinks. Turns out her dad is loaded, guess you have to be with that many siblings. It also explains why Charlie is best buddies with Pudding. She returns with three pints of Guinness. I can honestly say, I have never had it before in my life. The first few mouthfuls are hard to swallow. It's like drinking blood but after a while, I find the taste semi appealing. It's not as appetising as a lager and black but the darkness of it makes me feel somewhat mysterious and worldly. First, a rug muncher, then the 'it' crowd and now a Guinness. The life I once knew is definitely evaporating and I am happy with this.

Against all odds, I have had an enjoyable evening. Who knew that blowing a condom up on your head through your nostrils could be so funny. Also, who knew that having three pints of Guinness makes you shit bricks. By the time I come home to my digs, I am slightly pissed. I hug my new best friends. Even Charlie's hug has sentiment, at least I think that's what you call it when your new friend squeezes your arse cheek. Pudding and I are definitely besties. She loves her new nickname but it comes at a price; I am now known as Noodle. I flop onto my bed, fully clothed. I can't be arsed to take my wash bag to the communal bathroom and clean myself up. I am filled with fortified iron therefore I must be like the bionic woman right now and don't need to clean myself? I lay back happy. It's not quite what I expected for my first night at uni but somehow I know my time here will be awesome. I drift off into a deep sleep, dreaming about horses with hairy snatches and warriors riding on their backs – WTF?

The next few weeks of uni fly by. Before I know it, we are in December and it's almost the half term break. Pudding, Charlie and I have become good friends. Being able to do the splits after five pints, really helps to cement a friendship – who knew! It turns out I have a bit of a crush on my Business Law lecturer. He has one of those tweed jackets, scruffy shoes and a satchel that looks like it just wants to die in the graveyard of old satchels. I know exactly what Jeff will smell like. It will be something along the lines of stale bed sheets mixed with Brut and Head & Shoulders – I got a whiff the other day when he was handing out papers. I tried to snuffle up essence of stale sex but got caught out. Sadly, at the same point, a hall room fart bomb had been detonated and I think Jeff believed I was enjoying the pleasures of my own scent.

I never realised being at uni would make me so horny. I have had more wet dreams in these last few weeks than probably in my entire life – OK, maybe in the past twelve months but bloody hell. I struggle to understand why this is, perhaps it's the expectation/wishful thinking that I am going to get laid, any minute, any minute now, any time, I'm waiting... Except it just isn't happening – yet anyway. I have to be honest, I am a little disappointed. I thought I would have had at least two sexual encounters by now, but the truth is I've had zero. I don't know whether I am sending off the wrong signals or whether I'm just not considered totty material. What really surprises me and fucks me right off actually, is the fact that the fat, spotty, distasteful dress sense girl, two doors down from me is blowing kisses to some random bloke almost every other morning. I recognised one as the pizza delivery boy. OK, so that doesn't count but there was definitely a few from my class and Akbars, Pizza Hut do make really good pizzas. I bet she had no left overs.

After waking up from another amazing orgasmic wet dream about Jeff, I decide to make a pact with myself that I am going to get laid this weekend. I have to. I am going home next weekend and what will Jayne say? She is currently living vicariously so I have to have some juice to give her.

I decide to make a real effort today. It's Friday after all. Pudding and Charlie's classes finish the same time as mine and we are going to meet in the Union Bar. Normally, despite good intentions of heading into the city, we end up staying there, playing pool and drinking shots along with pints of Guinness. Then comes the usual kebab or tandoori pizza and I'm usually passed out on my bed, fully clothed sometime between the hours of one a.m. and two.

Tonight has to be different. If I am to get laid, we need to hit the city. I'm wearing Levi denim hot pants, a cropped top, my hair is down the middle of my back, my lips are totally berry and the black eye liner is giving a definite fuck me look. I decide to ditch the Doc Martens today and opt for the black stilettos my mother purchased for me (in case I went out for dinner). I never realised wearing stilettos made your calves look so muscular. As I leave my room, fat, spotty girl gives a wolf whistle. I pretend not to notice but deep down, I'm feeling it. I decide to get the lift (I need to check myself out in the mirror again). I'm the only one in. I lean my head to the side, flick my hair and start massaging my breasts. Without realising, we are at floor two and guess who should catch me flirting with myself? Bloody Jeff. I scurry to the back of the lift and start sticking my fingers into my teeth in an attempt to pretend that that's what I was doing, picking something out my tooth. I lean back against the back of the lift. Oddly enough, he looks more sheepish than me. He manages a quick, "Jess" but then seems a little nervous. It doesn't take me long (one floor to be exact) to realise what he has been up to. The dirty bastard. Shagging a student. He could get fired for that. However, the reality is I realise I am really pissed off that I am not the shagged student. I suddenly feel really betrayed. Doesn't he know I've been having hot, wet orgasms about him these past few weeks. In fact, didn't I get dressed up today in the hope of scoring Jeff?

When the lift pings to the ground floor, we both exit. Jeff marches off towards the lecturers' staff room. Somewhat despondently I head towards my 'Communication' lecture.

Thankfully, on my way I bump into Pudding who is on her way to some other lecture to do with ankle biters.

"Whey hey there, Mrs, someone is looking hot." She presses her finger against my arm and makes a sizzle sound. "Got a date tonight, have we?" she asks, rather giddily.

"Yes, and you are it." She looks at me slightly perplexed but eager as chuff as always. "I need to get laid," I say. "We've got to head into the city tonight Pud (she gets abbreviated occasionally).

"Awesome," she replies. "I'll tell Charlie." That's what I need, I think to myself. Friends who you can just be completely honest with and they will do what you need them to when in times of need.

I'm late for my lecture. The doors to the building are so old that it makes a racket when I open it. Everyone turns to stare. Some stare longer than socially acceptable. My communication lecturer, Mr Taylor, has been particularly pleasant this lecture. He's probably as old as Trevor and has the ability to avoid all eye contact and talk purely to your chest. However, he allowed me to sit out of the discussion exercise today. When I told him I was on a special 'communication mission' tonight and winked, he winked back. He suggested I sit at the back and catch up on my business homework. When the class ends, I head straight to the girls' toilet. I check myself out in the mirror and reapply my make-up. OK, so I may look a little too desperate, but the truth is, I am. I need some action tonight and it can't involve Jeff, my old headmaster, my cousin, Lisa or Mr Taylor (the sleeping brain works in mysterious ways).

I head straight to the Union Bar. I'm the first there. I order three drinks (just to prove I have friends) and go hide away in the corner. I'm getting some odd looks. In fact, one guy is licking around the rim of his pint glass. Disgusting. I try to pull down my hot pants a little lower so I'm not showing as much leg but it's a fruitless task. What would my mother say, I wonder? Probably something along the lines of "slap a saddle on you and you'll be the best ride in the county!"

I shake my head, I need to stop these thoughts. The reality is, I am out for one thing tonight, to get what I want/need so I have to look the part. I start filing my nails on the rough edge of the table and start considering what music I will play on the juke box, East 17's, *It's All right* just ain't doing it. I am feeling the need for Colour Me Badd, *I wanna sex you up*. Just as I am inserting my twenty pence, Pudding and Charlie arrive. When I turn around, Pudding is stood there wearing almost the same outfit as me, though the crop top is a little longer. She looks like a four-year-old has applied her black eye liner but you can't blame a girl for trying. Charlie looks me up and down and I swear she flushes.

"Forget to get dressed this morning?" she says, trying to be funny and it would be if she wasn't snorting and fake laughing too much. I gesture to their drinks at the table and we sit down.

Pudding raises her glass, "Here's to Jess getting laid tonight," she toasts. I down the remainder of my pint and sit impatiently waiting for them to finish their drinks. Pudding, clearly aware I am wanting to get out of here, does her best to neck hers. Meanwhile, Charlie is taking small sips. It's been almost a whole three minutes and she has only drunk three fingers full. God she can be irritating. I shuffle about a bit in my seat. Not because the hot pants are giving me a wedgy but because I need to hit the city.

"You two get another," suggests Charlie, who is still painstakingly sipping her drink.

"How about you drink up," I say in the hope she will get the message. She sits back.

"I hate this music," she says getting up and heading for the juke box. I look at Pud, she shrugs her shoulders. I can't cope. I need to get into the city. I have totty to find. Whilst Charlie is at the juke box, I head to the bar. Ten seconds later, I return with one of the take a pint out cartons. I pour Charlie's ¾ pint into the carton. Pud gives me an approving nod. Sashaying to Shakespeare's Sister, *Stay*, Charlie returns to the table.

"Where the fuck is my drink," she asks. I hold up the carton.

"Come on, the number ten bus will be here in five, we will be in the city for five thirty p.m., just in time for the suits to finish work," I say smiling. Targeting the after-work brigade is never a disappointment. They usually get pissed really quickly, share their hard-earned cash on buying drinks for the ladies and will usually shag anything that even looks their way. That's what Jayne told me anyway. Pudding practically bounces out the door. Begrudgingly, Charlie follows behind like a petulant child, carton in hand.

We make the bus and get dropped off just near the Corn Exchange. It's surrounded by bars and the music is pumping out. The suits are starting to arrive. I guide us to the bar which appears to have the most suits. There are tables and chairs outside the bar. As we walk past, I latch onto my first set of fuck me eyes. He's staring, I'm staring. He stands up, he knocks the tables and spills his friend's drink all over the floor. As he swaggers over to me, I realise I've made a big mistake with this one.

"Ess up gorgeous. Whasss your name?"

"Tinkerbell," says Charlie, shoving him into another set of tables behind him. Fuck. The couple sat at the table don't look impressed. As we head towards the bar, the barman is shaking his head. Bollocks, we have to leave.

"Crap bar anyway," I say as we leave the bar. We head to the next one, a few doors down. There aren't as many people at this one. We order our drinks. I order a large white wine, I'm trying to avoid the student look. We go and sit down outside. I'm happy. I love being out and about in the city. It's exciting. Who knows who I might meet. I'm like a dog on heat. Every man that walks past, I stare at. I finish my white wine and go order another round. Lord knows how much it will cost me, but I don't care tonight. I have a stash of Pot Noodles which will see me through until I go home. Food can wait, this is important. Whilst I wait to be served, a handsome suit comes to my side. He's definitely older than me, quite a bit older actually but who's counting.

"I saw you walk in," he says.

"Thanks," I reply. Thanks – what the hell? He smiles.

"Those your friends?" he asks, nodding in the direction of Pudding and Charlie.

"Yep," I reply, not knowing what else to say.

"You make an interesting group," he says. His eyes are twinkling now.

"Interesting?" I ask.

"Well," he says, clearing his throat, "here's the stunner, then we have the lesbian and the desperate one." I thought I was the desperate one, I wonder to myself.

"Makes an interesting mix," he adds.

"£9.40," says the barman. Crap, it's expensive here.

"Allow me," says the suit.

"Thanks," I reply, not wishing to look a gift horse in the mouth. We stand and chat at the bar. He's an insurance broker, single though the tan line on his ring finger tells a different story. He's funny. I like him.

"Where you heading next," he asks.

"I've no idea," I truthfully reply.

"Ravens," he says. "That's where everyone goes."

"Ace," I say.

He smiles, "Ace," he replies and heads back to his group of friends. Ace – who the hell says ace these days? I head back to Charlie and Pud.

"Ooohh he's dead fit," says Pud. Once again, she's doing that bouncing thing. I start to wonder if this was a bad idea but then I look across and the suit is smiling at me. I smile back.

"Where next?" asks Charlie, who has now entered the Olympic Games for downing a pint.

"Erm, I don't know, maybe Ravens," I suggest, pretending I've picked it out of my head.

"It's too early for Ravens," she says. "The Two Dolphins," she says like we have any choice.

"But," I try to protest.

"Don't worry, we will go to Ravens afterwards and you can meet up with Mr Fucking It." Oh, I do hope he is Mr Fucking It, I think to myself.

We seem to be walking a long time and I am beginning to think Charlie is taking us back to the Union Bar. However, as we head down another back alley I can hear music booming out. It's not music I recognise. There's a beat, well more of a thud and it sounds like there is groaning mixed in. I check my watch. It's seven p.m. Great, we will have one in here then head to Ravens.

When we arrive at the pub, I'm surprised to see a small queue outside. I look ahead and the entire Addams Family reunion is stood outside. I have never seen so many tattoos and piercings in one place before. I imagine a magnet coming down here and wrenching every fucker onto it.

"Fuck this," says Charlie. Great, we aren't staying, I think. She heads up to the door. I watch her embrace some bloke. She's then waving us over. We head to the front of the queue. It's not a man at the front; I'm not really sure what it is, except it's wearing leathers and has a chain attached to its neck. Charlie whispers something into its ear. It laughs and grabs Charlie's snatch – err, gross, I think to myself. Pud and I follow Charlie in. I check on Pudding to make sure she is OK. What I love about this girl is no matter where you take her or who you put her with, she is completely at home. She's clapping her hands, wiggling her arse and heading to the bar. I wish I could be more like Pudding. I look around. This place isn't normal. There are men and woman in cages with leather masks on their heads. There are no normal couples, well, to define, there are no mixed couples i.e. boy and girl, it's just girl and girl and boy and boy. I try to pretend I am not glaring as we walk past two girls who are French kissing. As I walk past, they turn their heads towards me but don't stop kissing. I can't deny it's a little intimidating. As we head to the bar, I realise I desperately need to pee. Why now? Charlie is ordering our drinks. She orders me a pint for which I am grateful, somehow a glass of Chardonnay in here won't go down well.

"I really need to pee," I say, hoping she will come with me.

"Straight down there," she says, pointing to close to where we walked in. Bollocks.

"Pud, do you need the lav?" I ask, praying she says yes.

"I'm fine, thanks," she replies. She's flirting with some gay guy at the bar who is wearing more make-up than she is.

I brave it alone and head back past the same couples and cages I just walked past. I make a conscious effort not to look anywhere but straight ahead. Keep your eye on the door, I tell myself. When I reach the ladies, I'm amazed to see there is no queue which is surprising considering this place is mainly filled with women. I go straight into a cubicle. After finishing, I give my hands a thorough wash. (I always need a poo on a night out, what's that about?) Stood at the side of me is a tall blond woman. I try not to take too much notice but as she leans into the mirror

I notice she has what looks like an Adams apple. I can't help but stare. She turns and stares back. Jeez. That is one ugly shim. Shim shrugs her/his shoulders and pretends to be bashful. What the chuff? I quickly grab some paper towels and dry my hands, ready to run out but then I feel a strong grip on my arm.

"Hiya, love," Shim says.

"Err."

"Here alone?" Shim asks.

"Err, no, I'm with my friend, my girlfriend," I say.

"Oh, shame," says Shim, "you're a straight man's dream." Shim's grip loosens and I quickly head out of the toilet. Thank fuck for that. I head back to the bar but I can't see Charlie or Pudding anywhere. Crapsticks. Where are they? I look around trying not to leave the spot. If I venture off course, I may get lost forever and turn into some pierced to the eyeballs lesbian. It's then I recognise a familiar shadow. I see Pudding's golden hair sashaying about. Thank chuff for that. I head over to Pudding. She's sat at a table with a load of others.

"Pud," I ask.

"Jess," she replies. "Come, meet my new friends. OK, so this is Henry and Henry's partner, Michael."

"Hiya," comes a gay chorus.

"Hi," I reply.

"And this is Jonathan and Boris. They just met tonight, isn't that lovely?"

"Fabulous," I reply. "Where's Charlie?" I ask, desperate to get out of here.

"Oh, she went off into the cloakroom down there," she says, pointing towards a door.

The boys snigger. "Gobblers alley," says Henry. Michael squeezes his knee. Fucking hell, selfish bitch, I think. How dare she be getting some action when it's my night for some action.

She's had plenty since she arrived at uni. It's amazing how many drunk girls are into a bit of female action when it's last orders.

"Jess, Boris has some special cake," says Pud.

"No thanks," I reply. "I don't do poppers."

"It's not poppers," says Boris. "It's cake, homemade."

"It tastes amazing," says Pud.

"What, you've had some?" I ask, amazed that Pud could be so trusting.

"It's just a brownie," says Pud. "It's divine." Boris unwraps a baking sheet filled with chocolate brownies. Wow. They do look amazing. "Go on Jess, just try some, it's gorgeous," she says. What the hell, I think. Since we may be here a while and I am rather peckish but just a nibble, I say to myself. I sit down in the half moon seats with the rest of them.

Two slices later and I'm feeling pretty spectacular. I love our new friends, we all keep telling each other. I've lost count of how many Chardonnay's I've had but it turns out my new best friend Boris loves Chardonnay just as much as I do. Pudding is hilarious. She's managed to grow a huge tit on the side of her cheek. She's obsessed with it and keeps checking the mirrored walls. I'm fairly certain she's always had it, we just never mentioned it before. Thankfully, Michael makes her feel at ease. When he points out his third arm, we giggle a lot. He and Pudding were made for each other, three tits and three arms – they could name a pub after them. The giggling continues, in fact, we can't stop giggling. It's at this point Charlie joins us.

"What the fuck have you two being doing?" she says, snatching the empty baking paper. "I can't leave you anywhere."

"Uh oh, it's the grumpy muncher, monster muncher," I laugh now hysterically at my own joke. We are all laughing. Pudding can't stop.

"For fucks sake," says Charlie. She grabs Pud and me by the arms and yanks us out of the bar. We are still laughing but protesting that we haven't been able to say bye to our new friends. I try to take my arm back but it feels like jelly. When we get outside the fresh air smacks me around the face. I stop giggling. I look at Charlie. She seems really tall, like really, really tall, so does Pudding and her snatch. It's in front of me now. Pudding has lowered herself down and is having a massive wee. It's like a river.

"We are all going to die," I shout. Whack. Charlie smacks me across the face. "What did you do that for?" I ask. Suddenly, she's a normal size again.

"Come on," she says. "We are going back to the Union."

"No," I say. My feet stay firmly on the spot. In fact, I think they are glued into the concrete.

"No," says Pudding, equally as firmly. We hold hands in union.

"Fine," says Charlie but you two are having water."

"Ravens, lead the way bitch," I say, pretending to be all sergeant major like. Pudding looks at me and we both explode into a fit of giggles. Charlie is staring now. She looks a bit scary, I think I can see fire in her eyeballs.

"Listen, if we are going anywhere else you two need to get your act together or else they won't let us in, you hear." We salute and giggle some more. Charlie curses and starts walking ahead. Pudding and I follow arm in arm. As we head back to the main area of bars, Pudding and I manage to get it together. Charlie stops us just outside Ravens.

"Right you two, straighten up, stop smiling and let go of each other." We do as she says.

Pudding whispers, "You need to get laid, I need to get you laid, you need I need to get laid." I nod. I fully understand everything she has just said.

Amazingly, we are allowed into Ravens. It's an old warehouse that has three floors and is the cutting edge of bars. It's very minimalist. Charlie sits us down on a bench just near a large glass table whilst she goes and gets us our drinks. There is a huge mirror opposite us. I look into the mirror, Pudding's third tit is still there but there is something else, something is floating around my head. I look about but can't see it. I check the mirror again. It's there again, it has wings. I reach to catch it but keep missing. I keep checking the mirror, eventually I have it in my palm. I can feel it fluttering about.

"Pudding, Pudding, look, I've got something," I say. I slowly release my fingers to reveal the most beautiful fairy I have ever seen. I think I am going to cry. "Look Pud, isn't she, she's so beautiful."

"Oh, how pretty, I want one," she says.

"There," I point, noticing another one flying around. Pudding grabs it and we both stare in awe at our fairies. Without realising, there is a figure stood in front of me.

"Hiya gorgeous," says some man in a suit. I look up. Oh, it's him from earlier. Yes, I remember, my shag. Perfect.

"Hi," I say, looking at him but then straight back to check my fairy.

"You OK there, love?"

"Oh yes," I say. "I've never been better. Look, meet Filo, my fairy." The suit looks at me and looks at my hand. He looks quizzically. "What you talking about, love? There's nothing there."

"Yeah, right, she's right here. Look, she just curtsied at you." Charlie walks over now.

"Is your friend all right?" he asks.

"She's fine," Charlie abruptly responds, placing two pint glasses of water in front of Pudding and me.

"What's she taken?" he asks.

"Nothing," replies Charlie.

"Cake," says Pudding. "We've had cake, brownie cake, mmmmm." The suit nods.

"I see," he says. He sits down next to me. "She's lovely," he says gesturing to my fairy. I smile, pleased he likes my fairy as much as I do. He places his hand on my knee. I don't really notice when it starts going higher and higher until he is near my knickers.

"Get off her," shouts Charlie. The suit ignores Charlie and starts nibbling at my neck. It tickles, I giggle. "I said get the fuck off her," says Charlie. She is stood up now. The suit dismisses her with his hand. Charlie grabs him by the scruff of his neck onto his feet.

"Fuck you, bitch," says the suit. He shoves Charlie into the table behind us. I don't know what to do about this. I can't let go of my fairy but I need to help Charlie. The suit is starting to sit down again next to me but before he gets chance to sit, Charlie is on his back. He screams. She's bitten his ear. Everything then happens really quickly. There are people around us, more men in suits. I can see Charlie being air lifted out of the bar. Pud and I are grabbed by some more men in suits with ear pieces. Before I know, we are thrown out on the street.

"My fairy," I yell. I can't find my fairy. Pudding has lost hers too. She is crawling around on the floor looking for it. I start to cry. Charlie grabs my arm and yanks me up.

"Come on, we need to get out of here before the police arrive." The police, I need the police, they will help me find my fairy. I resist. "Jess, get a fucking grip. There is no fairy, you are

stoned. Get your shit together or else we are going to get nicked."
I want to resist her but what she is saying somehow makes sense.
Charlie helps Pud to stand up and leads us both to the taxi station.

Fifteen minutes later we are sat back in the Union Bar. My
head feels fuzzy. I keep drinking the water Charlie is giving me.
I suddenly have a massive urge for sugar.

"I need sugar," I announce. Pudding has her head on the
table. She is groaning.

"That was very bad cake," she says. I walk over to the bar
and buy three chocolate bars and a large full fat coke. This should
sort me out. Charlie is sat looking really, really pissed off. As the
drugs finally start to wear off, I then realise that I failed to
succeed in my task of getting laid. I feel really depressed.

"You OK, hun?" asks Pud, who no longer has a tit growing
out of her cheek.

"No, I'm not," I say. "All I wanted was a shag." Pudding
places her arms around my shoulders and I lean in, pretending to
fake sob.

"Oh, for fucks sake, it's not like it's the night before the
apocalypse. You can have any one you want, Jess. You're just
too damn picky."

"I'm not picky," I say.

"Err, I think you are. Aren't you always on the hunt for
another rock God?"

"No," I defensively respond, regretting telling her about my
night with Mickey. "I just want to meet the right person. I've to
find them attractive or else I might…"

"You might what?" goads Charlie.

"I might not orgasm," I sheepishly reply.

"Oh, for fucks sake, Jess, you shouldn't need to rely on a
man to give you an orgasm. Can't you do it yourself."

"Of course I can," I lie. The truth is, I haven't been able to achieve an orgasm on my own. I laid in the bath for almost two hours once, fumbling about trying to climax, it just didn't happen.

"I could give you an orgasm in about sixty seconds," laughs Charlie. I stare at her.

"No, you can't," I reply, laughing back. She leans in, looking deadly serious.

"You are so naïve, Jess. Of course I can, I'm something of an expert in the field," she sniggers. I stare at her, wondering if she really could give me an orgasm in sixty seconds. I grab her pint and knock back the contents.

"Go on then," I say. She is staring at me now. Pudding is looking confused. Charlie stands up, I feel my stomach flip. She senses my nervousness and sits back down.

"Don't worry, Jess, it will happen. Get Pud to buy you a dildo." She looks a little annoyed. I get up and head over to the bar. I return to the table with a tray of shots.

Pudding groans, "I don't think I can do that," she says and burps up a bit of brownie. I stare at Charlie, "Cheers," I say clinking her shot glass with mine. Three shots later I am feeling numb. Pudding is asleep at the table.

"Come on then," I say, holding out my hand to Charlie. "Let's do this." She studies me a minute, then stands up.

"We need to get Pud back first," she says. Somehow, despite feeling like I'm floating, I manage to assist Charlie in guiding Pudding out of the bar. We walk across to the residence, not saying a word. When we reach Pud's floor, Charlie takes out the key from Pud's purse and gives her a little push into her room. Thud. Pud lands flat on the floor. She groans.

"She's OK," says Charlie. We head back to the lift. I'm staggering a little; the mixture of hash and shots is taking its effect. I really need to sit down. We get back into the lift. Charlie presses six, my floor. I press eight, her floor. If we are doing this, we are doing it in her room. I don't want my fellow sixth floor occupants witnessing anything. Charlie's floor is used to women coming and going out of her room.

When we reach Charlie's room, she unlocks the door and holds it open for me to walk in. I manage to move my feet a bit further and head straight for the bed, plonking myself down.

"Are you OK, Jess?" she asks, a little concerned now.

"I'm fine," I say, slurring back.

"Sit," I order, patting the bed. Charlie takes off her biker boots and sits down next to me. She just sits there and doesn't move an inch. I lean towards her and start kissing her. She doesn't respond and pulls back.

"Are you sure you want to do this, Jess?" she asks with genuine concern.

"I've never wanted anything more in my life," I say and place my hand on her snatch. She removes my hand and then pushes me back on the bed. She pins my arms above my head and then leans in and kisses me. It's a soft kiss and it feels rather good. I can feel her tongue piercing. I'm enjoying this, more than I thought. I feel a rush of adrenaline. I release my arms from her grip and reach for her tits. She lets out a little groan but then grabs my arms again, holding them back above my head. She uses one hand to hold both my arms whilst the other eases its way down my body. Her hand is on my hot pants. She is gently pressing and caressing my snatch. It feels so good. I arch my back and groan.

"You have an amazing body," she says. Her tongue is gliding over my navel whilst her other hand continues to press on my hot pants. Wow, this feels incredibly good. She tugs down the pants and delicately slips her hand into my knickers. She groans when she feels how moist I am. She pulls down my pants.

Her fingers then start stroking my clitoris. She applies a small amount of pressure then stops. It feels so good and I can feel an orgasm building. Her other hand now lifts up and she pulls up my bra. She places her lips on my nipple which immediately responds. She starts teasing it, nibbling and sucking it, whilst her other hands continues to tease my clitoris. I groan. I can't contain it, I allow the pressure to release and have a full-blown orgasm. My body jerks. She takes her hands off my clitoris but keeps her hand on my snatch, pressing harder which sends me into another frenzy. I can't keep still. It's becoming too much, I want her hand there but it's sending me into some orgasmic overload. She eventually withdraws, as if reading my thoughts and I relax, huffing and puffing with a lot of, "Oh my's." Just when I think that's it, her head is between my legs and she is licking me. Her piercing is scraping around my clitoris. Oh crap, I can feel myself building again. This is amazing. It doesn't take me long to reach climax again. After this one, I feel tired, really tired, like I can't keep my eyes open any longer tired...

I wake with a start. Where am I? What the hell happened? Someone is next to me. I turn and see Charlie is in bed next to me, naked. Then it hits me and I begin to remember. Holy fuck, I think to myself. I daren't move a muscle. My arm is laid against her back. I debate chewing it off rather than waking her. I can't face dealing with this right now. I gently manage to ease my arm away and delicately glide myself out of bed. I grab my knickers and head for the door. I quietly open it and as I leave, I turn back. She is mumbling and shuffling about in the bed so I close the door. I have no idea what time it is or what I look like. It's quiet on the floor though so I'm hoping it's still early.

I decide to take the stairs, rather than risk bumping into someone. As I reach my floor, I peek my head around the corner first to make sure no one is around. Nothing. I quietly tiptoe to the end of the corridor. Why does my room have to be the furthest away? Just as I am two doors from my room, I hear a door behind me open. Shit. I freeze. I don't know what to do. I turn. Stood there, fastening his belt, is Jeff. Ah, so that's who he is shagging. But wait, that's Lou's room. Quiet, barely speaks Lou. Jeff turns and sees me looking. He looks back and a sly smile creeps on his face whilst looking me up and down. I smile back. He then "Sshh's" me and winks. It's our secret. Phew – but wait, I haven't done anything wrong, or that he knows anyway. Just then the door opens again and out pops Nadia from my business group. She is tucking her shirt into her jeans. She stops and stares at me. Her expression says it all.

"Ssshh," I whisper back and carry on to my room. Well, who knew, dirty filthy bitch that Lou I think. When I enter my room, I check the clock. It's five forty-five a.m. I've had about four hours sleep. My head is banging. I go to the bathroom to get some water. When I look in the mirror, I don't recognise my reflection. My skin is positively glowing, my hair looks like it's home to about fifty pigeons and I have mascara running down my cheeks. I open my mouth to drink the water and almost gag at the smell of my breath.

After brushing my teeth, I strip and climb into bed. What the hell happened last night? How did I end up with Charlie? I then remember the brownies and the bar where we got thrown out. It's all making sense. I recall being in the Union Bar and the challenge I set for Charlie. Wow. Does hash bring out my inner lesbian? I then remember the mind-blowing orgasms I had. At first, I cringe, embarrassed, but then reflect that it was actually pretty amazing. Not so amazing that I ever want to repeat it, but one for the record. How am I going to face Charlie again? I'll die of embarrassment. Didn't I fall asleep on her? In fact, I don't recall giving her any pleasure back. How selfish of me. Not that

I would know what to do, given I can't even make myself have an orgasm.

I close my eyes. My head can't deal with all this right now. I manage to drift off into a deep sleep. I am woken to loud banging. It's at my door. "Jess, Jess, are you in there?" It's Pudding. I climb out of bed and throw my dressing gown around me. I open the door.

"Oh good, you are here. I was worried. I can't remember a thing about last night. What happened?" Pudding sits on my bed and I recount the evening. She appears to have lost memory of most of the evening but then she did have more brownie than me. We start giggling again and laugh at the fairies and the third tit.

"What happened to Charlie?" she asks.

"Erm, she just went back to her room. You know, she saw us home then I guess went back to her room," I say, trying to sound convincing.

"Oh right," says Pud, looking at me with a quizzical look.

The last week before half term flies by. I manage to avoid Charlie for the most part. I briefly saw her across the canteen but quickly engaged myself in conversation with Phil Butters about the advertising project we are working on. When Friday arrives, I pack up my things and head straight for the station. Trevor is picking me up from Wakefield Westgate. My mum insisted he pick me up from uni, but I lied and told her I had some errands to run in Wakefield first. I don't need my mum and step-dad collecting me. I'm not twelve any more.

Chapter Twelve
June 1996

It's over. Four years at uni vanished. Where on earth did that go? I'm surrounded by boxes. I'm packed. I've sat my last exam and I am heading home. I've given notice at the Union Bar. The only thing I am pleased about it all coming an end. I couldn't bear another night working there. It's so depressing watching everyone else get shit faced on a weekend when I have to work.

I head down to the kitchen. My house mates, Lou and Faye, are eating breakfast. They've become my best, lifelong mates. Lou and I had a lot in more in common than we both realised. Turns out she's not the quiet, shy type. As for Faye, I met her at a crazy house party. We both recorded the same time on the bucking bronco and a friendship formed. After a few nights out together, our friendship was cemented. I still see Pud every now and again. However, she fell head over heels with a guy named Oliver so isn't much up to partying any more. She proudly told me she has had three kidney infections from all the shagging she's been doing. Good for her, I think. As for Charlie, we are cool. She has a steady girlfriend. It took some time before I could look her in the eyes again, well, without going beetroot red. When I tried to bring it up once, she just shrugged her shoulders and said, "Told you, sixty seconds," then changed the subject.

I've managed to have a few sexual encounters in the past four years, aside from Charlie. I lowered the bar somewhat and so experienced my fair share of men. Most were nothing to write home about. There was one guy, Ted, who I really liked, I even thought I might be in love with him. We went out for about a month. It ended when I caught him getting a blow job in the women's toilets at the Union Bar. I'm currently single and totally fine with that. I'm fortunate to have a fuck buddy who I can call on when I get the urge, Chris. We have a pact that if either of us don't pull and are in need, we can call on each other. I've only called him once, he's knocked quite a few more times and even though it can be silly o'clock in the morning, I don't mind. The sex is actually really good. He knows what I like. I don't really fancy him, though alcohol definitely helps me drink him pretty.

"So, this is it," I say. Faye is layering marmite over her toast so every inch is covered. Gross. The smell makes me gag.

"Aye up," says Faye. "We were just talking about you." I can feel the lump build in my throat.

"Anyway, girls, so like I'm off soon, so you know, thought we could you know, cry or something." Before the words have left my mouth I am embraced with arms, chests, hairs and a very distinct smell of marmite.

"Don't worry mate, this isn't the end. It's just the start."

When I open the door, I hear a screech. "She's here. Ahhh, Jess, come here, love, give me a squeeze." My mother throws her arms around me. "You're too skinny," she says. Of course I am, I think. I've been on a diet of beer, Chardonnay and Pot Noodles for the past four years, what does she expect? Trevor starts bringing in my stuff from the car.

"Sorry I couldn't come to help but my back has really been playing up. So, what's the plan then?" she asks, before my foot is barely through the door. Getting out of out this hell hole I think but obviously don't say.

"Well, Mum, I've applied for a few jobs, I have a few interviews and then hopefully, you know, I'll be out of your hair."

"Out of my hair? I've just got you back, there's no need to rush off. However, I was hoping to turn your room into a sewing room." No pressure then, I think. I watch as she is "mming" me, clearly taking no notice, she's far too busy watching Trevor bring in all my crap. Clearly, the doting, weeping mother that left me four years ago has vanished. The look on her face as Trevor brings in all my belongings suggests that a massive turd has just landed on her lounge floor.

"Not there, Trevor, put those ones in the garage." I defensively reach for my box marked clothes. "Jessica, they need burning. They stink of cigarettes, beer, kebabs and Lord only knows what else. We will go shopping; my treat." There is no point arguing.

I head up to my room but it feels different. It doesn't feel like my room any more. The fact that there is a stack of neatly folded fabric laying on my cabinet has nothing to do with it. My mother barges in.

"Oh, let me take this away. I was just getting ready for you, err, you know, anyway, you'll find everything is in order. I took down your posters when Trevor painted the room. Do you like the duck egg blue? It's much better than the purple, don't you think?" I nod. After Trevor delivers the last of the few items that are allowed into my room, I sit on my bed. My belongings sit in that one holdall and a box. They represent the past four years of my life. I lay back against the duck egg blue scatter cushion. Having spent the last eighteen years of my life in this room, it no longer represents me and who I am. I stupidly thought that coming home would be easy; I'd just move back in and all would be as it was. I even thought my mum might be pleased to have me home but watching her hover about as I squash her matching duck egg cushion, which matches the duck egg curtains, I can sense I am spoiling the look. To confirm this, as soon as I get up off the bed, she starts fluffing the cushions. I tut, slightly louder than I intended.

"Don't you be tutting at me when you get your own place, you'll want your things in order too, you know."

"Yes, Mother," I reply. I start to make my way downstairs.

"Aren't you going to unpack?" she asks.

"Later," I call back. This has the exact effect I was hoping for; she is unpacking my stuff. She can't bear my tatty holdall and box on her new duck egg blue rug.

I head into the kitchen, promising myself I will get out of here soon before I turn into one of those Laura Ashley dressing stiffs. Trevor is in there washing grease off his hands.

"So, what do you think to the duck egg then?" he asks, with a gleam in his eye.

"It's like the Easter bunny has come and shat all over the room," I reply. He chuckles. It's the first time in a long time that I have seen him chuckle.

"It's our bedroom next, you know. She's picked wallpaper with birds on it. Oriental, she says. Think she got the idea from the local Chinese take-away." We both giggle. I sense Trevor is pleased to have me back.

"So, what are your plans, Jess. Heading to Australia or getting a job?"

"Getting a job," I reply. "Australia will have to wait."

"That's a shame," says Trevor. "You always talked about going there, thought you might one day."

"Yeah, well, that's when you can still dream. Reality is, I owe the equivalent deficit of a small country."

He smiles. "It gets easier, Jess," he says, resting his hand on my shoulder. "Don't give up your dreams." He walks out of the kitchen, leaving me stunned. That has to be the most heart-warming conversation I have had with anyone, ever, let alone bloody Trevor.

If I thought I had the summer to chill out before I hopefully get a job, I was mistaken. I've been home approximately forty-eight hours and the *Yorkshire Post* is ringed in large red circles and stuffed under my nose.

"It's always good to have a back-up plan, love. Not to say you won't get the job, but you know, it doesn't hurt to have a back-up." I glare at my mother. This is the woman who briefly worked in the doctors' surgery for six months. She managed to get herself sacked for diagnosing too many patients. If she'd had put more effort into her career than finding a new husband, she'd be a self-made millionaire.

My interview is tomorrow at the biggest confectionary factory in the UK. There is nothing quite like a Teri tree chocolate. I've managed to keep my mother at arm's length whilst I 'prepare'. Not that there is anything to prepare for. I am who I am; I passed my exams, my lecturers said some good things about me. What else is there to do? Whilst she is out shopping, I take the opportunity to sprawl out on her wicker sun lounger, pour myself a G&T and listen to Jamiroquai at full volume. Within seconds of my head hitting the pillow, the phone rings.

"Jessica, it's me. Thought I would just remind you to hang out the washing, since most of it's yours. Peg it out and I'll iron it later."

"Yes, Mother," I reply.

"What's that racket in the background?" she asks.

"Oh, just my music."

"How can you prep for your meeting with that racket?"

"Erm, it's just what us students do, kinda of used to it. Is that it?" I ask, feeling irritated.

"Yes, I'll be back later. I'm meeting Janet for a spot of lunch so will be later than planned." Get in, I think to myself.

I head back to the sun lounger, passing the washing machine. I will hang it out in a bit. The phone rings again. Oh, for fucks sake, I think to myself.

"Hello."

"And can you get the lamb chops out to defrost, I forgot this morning," says my mother.

"Where are you calling from?"

"The phone box. Why? Does it matter? Just do it, will you?"

"Fine, can I go now?"

"Just keep the place tidy, will you. I don't want to come home to a mess. Bye." She hangs up. Bloody woman. Her OCD has taken itself to a whole new level since I left for uni. I throw the chops on the counter in full sun, so they will defrost quicker. Just as I am about to lay down, the phone rings again.

"Arrrghh." I shout. "What now? Put down the toilet seat, wash your hands, brush your teeth, honestly…"

"Well, you can do that if you like but it's not what I rang for…"

"Oh, sorry, thought you were, erm, who is this?"

"It's me, Faye, you daft bat. Having some home trouble?" she asks.

"My bloody mother, get me out of here," I beg.

"Well it just so happens that's why I am ringing. So, my Auntie Carole was supposed to be going on holiday to Newquay on Saturday and has booked an apartment opposite Fistral Beach. However, my uncle has taken a turn for the worst and they can't go. She's offered the place to me instead, for half the price. What do you think? Two weeks in Newquay. Thought I'd ask you first. I know Lou is going batty being back at home so I reckon she will be up for it." I can't speak, I'm speechless, in fact I think I'm hyperventilating I am so frigging excited.

"Jess, Jess, you there, you OK?" We spend the next one hour sorting out the details. Faye has checked the trains and we can get a train down there at midnight from Wakefield Westgate, arriving at eight a.m. on Saturday morning. There is only one slight hitch; I am supposed to have another job interview next week at some shipping company over in Hull. It doesn't take me long to convince myself that I know absolutely bugger all about boats and therefore, I am probably doing us both a favour by not attending. I immediately head upstairs and start to pack. I remember how much I love Newquay and then think of Pete, my first true love.

Trevor wakes me up at six thirty a.m. as I requested. My head is still banging from the huge argument I had with my mother last night. OK, so I forgot to put the washing out and perhaps it was reckless to leave the chops in the full sun so they went off, but hey, I had important things on my mind. It was no big deal, she didn't need to be such a cow over it. I thought telling her I was off to Newquay for two weeks would be welcomed. However, she freaked at that. I had to lie and pretend my interview had been postponed. She reckoned I was not taking the "finding a job thing" seriously enough. Apparently, it's not all fun and parties and going out with my friends; I have to buckle down, otherwise I might end up pregnant. I don't think me pointing out that's exactly what she did went down too well. She stormed upstairs slamming each door she passed. She's such a drama queen.

I put on the suit my mother bought me from C&A. It's a size too big and the arms come down past my hands, but it will do. I scrape my hair onto the top of my head to make myself look professional. The truth is, I really want this job. The perks are supposed be awesome and not just because you can eat as much chocolate as you like. The money is good and there is the added bonus that it's based in one of my all-time favourite places, aside from Newquay of course, York. There is no way I would commute; I would find a place to rent and be free of the ball and chain that is my mother. I imagine myself sitting in the Minster on a Saturday afternoon, reciting quotes from the greats. Or, maybe being on a Booze on the Ooze cruise – perhaps more my scene. However, I feel there is something that is drawing me to York and it's not just chocolate.

Seven hours later, I am back home. I yank off the suit jacket which sports the coffee stain I managed to get on the train on my way to the interview. I reflect back on the interview. I wasn't expecting to have to make a presentation and be put on the spot about a marketing idea. They could have warned me. I thought it would just be a chat, look around, check your papers and a nod and see you on your way. I felt like I was auditioning for a part on television. What was worse was the fact that you had to present to the other eight candidates who all looked more professional and had higher grades than me. However, I was secretly pleased with my proposed campaign for the new Terri tree fudge bar. Luckily for me, I had been listening to the Spice Girls on the train over. It therefore, didn't take me long to come up with, "I tell you what I want, what I really, really want, I really, really want a Teri tree fudge bar." My vision of dancing girls, singing into their fudge bars was quite unique or so I thought. It was far better than little Miss Clever Pants' version of a bear switching his honey for a fudge bar. Oh well, I think to myself. I'll just have to keep looking when I get back from Newquay.

A few days later…

My tongue is stuck to the roof of my mouth. The whole thing is as dry as a bone. I start to gag. I flap my arms around to see if there is a glass of water to hand. Bingo. I grab the glass, tip the contents down my neck but within seconds, blow it all back out again. That wasn't water. Tasted more like vodka. I groan. Oh man, I feel crap. My head is banging. My eyes are open now, I look around the room. It's a twin room. On the bed opposite I can make out Faye. She is fully clothed. I look down to see what I am wearing. I'm impressed I manage to put on my Pooh Bear nightie.

I can hear groaning and then the sound of something landing in water. Lou, poor thing, never could take her drink. After spotting the surf board above the bed with its carving, 'Easy Ride', reminds me I am in Newquay. We've been here for three nights and I can remember very little so far except for the amazing Fosters beer tent on Fistral Beach which supports the surfing competition. So far, our days have consisted of tanning/sleeping by day and partying hard at night. It all starts to come back to me now. I recall we were on the beach, there was music playing, lots of alcohol about and from the taste in my mouth, some weed, too.

"Water," I hear, "I need water," shouts Lou. Faye doesn't move an inch. I get up and head to the kitchen. Considering we haven't cooked a single thing since we arrived, the place is a shithole. There are glasses, ashtrays, take away pots everywhere. I quickly rinse out some orange looking stuff from the glass and pour some water for Lou. She grabs it out of my hands and downs it. Sixty seconds later, there is another splash at the bottom of the toilet again. I guess water isn't helping. I check the fridge to see if there is anything else I can give her. It's bare except for a four pack of beer, a bounty bar and a half-eaten pizza from two days ago. The milk carton is empty. Bollocks, no coffee. I can't function without my morning caffeine. There is only one thing for it; I'm going to have to nip to the shop. I check the clock; it's just after ten. Thankfully, the shop is just a few doors down from the apartment. Hardly anyone ever goes in there. I'll just pop down in my nightie I think. No one will bother. The guy who owns it looks half-dead anyway.

I slip on my Doc Marten boots and a pair of knickers. I splash my face with water, scrape my hair back with a bobble and grab my purse. I cypher my way past a bleached blond mass sleeping in our lounge area. I pause for a second, wondering if we are staying in some kind of shared chalet-type thing like you do when you go skiing (not that I've ever been – why would anyone want to spend that much money to exercise all day and get no tan?). However, the flashback of the previous evening dawns upon me and I realise these are our new best Ozzie friends. The ones who live in a VW camper van. Offering them floor space in a brick-type establishment was apparently like offering the keys to a room at the Four Seasons. I try to remember if I actually did anything with one of them but assure myself that there was no such evidence when I put on my knickers.

Two minutes later, I am out the door doing a mental shopping list. Coke, mini cheddars and Wotsits is Lou's secret hangover cure apparently. I take a quick glance around to see if anyone is about and then make a dash for the shop. I decide to allow myself three minutes to get there, get the stuff, pay and be back. I feel like Anneka Rice on *Challenge Anneka*.

I zoom down the aisle, grabbing items off the shelf as I pass. The smell of freshly baked French bread is lingering around the shop and sending my body into a frenzy. I need to stuff my face with some, certain it will cure my hangover. Stupidly, I didn't grab a basket. I shove all the items onto the counter. At a snail's pace, the almost dead owner taps each item into the till. I check my watch, I have got approximately thirty seconds left. I hand over the cash and grab the items. I haven't time to wait for his shaky hands to pull apart a shopping bag. I scoop up my items into my arms. The French stick is popping out just under my nose. I can barely see. I head to the door and smack straight into something. My nose feels like it's just exploded and the items have fallen out of my arms and are all over the floor.

"Youchey bollocks," I shout. My nose hurts. I realise I have been struck in the nose with the French baguette. As I remove my hands from my nose, I see they are covered in blood. "Fuck."

"Here," I hear someone say, a man.

"I'm so sorry." I can't focus, my eyes are watering too much from the pain in my nose. I am guided to a chair and told to sit. I am handed some paper towels and stuff these under my nose to help stop the bleeding.

"Tip your head back," says the man. I do as he asks. Some relief starts to come. My eyes aren't watering as much as I slowly start to focus. That's when I notice those blue sparkly eyes. I squint, checking, but each second my sight gets better, I realise it's him, it's Pete, my Pete, my first orgasm Pete.

"It's you," I say, like some doting fan.

"Err, yes, it's me, I broke your nose," he replies.

"No, it's you, Pete. You are Pete." He looks at me, staring at me for a minute. "Don't you recognise me?" I ask. He looks and then I realise what I must look like. Slowly I can see it is coming to him, I start to smile as he can see he recognises it's me.

"You remember me, right?" I ask proudly, pleased he remembers me.

"No, I really don't, I'm afraid," he replies.

"It's me, Jess, Jessica, summer of '89, Newquay, Ocean Wave Caravan Park, remember, me, you, a caravan...?" He is taking a minute.

"Jess, that Jess? Wow, how you've been?" He is smiling from ear to ear.

"Great, until about five minutes ago," I say.

"I can't believe it's you, fancy the chances of us meeting like this."

"Weird," I say.

"Couldn't write it," he replies. "Hang on, I tried to call you. You gave me a fake number," he says, his face now looking slightly annoyed.

"No, I didn't. My mum changed the number. Do you have any idea how many calls I made to B&B's in Bude trying to find you?" I ask.

"I was gutted," he says.

"Me too," I say. There is then an awkward moment.

"Pete, Peter, what the hell are you doing?" asks some rather attractive blond girl with hair down to her backside.

"This is Jess, Jess this is Caz." Caz looks me up and down like I am something that should be spat on. "I met Jess years ago. We were, err, well, anyway." Caz couldn't give a shit.

"We are late, Peter. We need to get going."

"Oh, right, yeah, well, err, are you OK? I mean, is your nose OK?" he asks, rather concerned.

"It will be fine, it's just bruised I think," I say, not really sure if it is bruised or broken. Pete helps me up to my feet and grabs my bits of food and places them in my arms. Caz leaves the shop heading towards a car parked outside.

"So, Jess," says Pete, walking me out of the door. "What you doing down here?"

"I'm on holiday with some uni friends," I say.

"Oh, great. How long for?"

"I leave in nine days," I say. "What about you," I ask.

"I'm on holiday here too. My girlfriend, I mean Caz and I, are down for a couple of weeks to watch the surf contest and do some surfing. Maybe we will see you about," he says.

"Sure," I say. "We are down the beach most days, you know, chilling and surfing." I have no idea why I said surfing.

"You surf now?" he asks.

"Sure," I say.

"Great, maybe we can catch a wave together. See you about, Jess," he says as we he walks towards the car. I can see Caz in the passenger seat glaring at me. Pete waves as he opens the door and drives off.

It takes me a few minutes to get my head around what just happened. When I open the apartment door, Lou screams. "What the hell happened to you?" she screeches before rushing back to the toilet. Over a breakfast of Coke, coffee, Wotsits and mini cheddars I tell them all about Pete, the '89 version and the recent meeting.

"Wow, I mean like, wow, this is massive, this is like the one, the one and only." We burst into a chorus of Chesney Hawkes. "But seriously Jess, Pete could be the one, your one true love." Faye's eyes look so dreamy as she says this. She's always liked the idea of being a hopeless romantic but the reality is, she just likes to be gagged and shagged up the arse.

"We need a plan, don't we, Lou?" says Faye. Lou is trying to nod but does it ever so delicately to ensure she doesn't throw up again. "We've got to get to the beach every day, you've got to look super-hot so he will dump that trumped-up tart, Caz, and run straight into your arms."

"I don't know if she is a trumped-up tart," I say.

"Oh, for fucks sake Jess, she's got your guy, right?"

"Right?"

"Well, fuck her. Mission is, Pete loves Jess for everrrrr. With me, Simkins?"

"Righto," I say, saluting Faye. I love the fact she has my back but she scares me a little too. She is so competitive and determined I sometimes wonder what she will do, to me in particular, if I don't get or do exactly what she asks.

We hit Fistral Beach. The first round of surfers is going out. We choose to position ourselves right in the thick of it. There is barely space to hang a hanky, let alone a towel but somehow, with Faye on the job, we secure ourselves a decent sizeable area to lay our towels. It takes less than one hour before Pete and Caz arrive on the beach. She's wearing one of those all in one swim suits that has a short skirt at the bottom, short enough so your arse cheeks peep through but long enough to make the hips look shapely. I'm in my vest top bikini and matching shorts. It's themed on the itsy bitsy teenie weenie yellow polka-dot bikini. The vest flatters my boobs, as for the shorts, they would look even better if for the fact that eating fast food and drinking too much beer wasn't starting to linger over the tight elastic waistband. Hey ho, I suck in.

Pete has his surf board with him. There is an area further down from the competition where you can surf. I watch him wax his board. I notice there are two boards, one more girlie-looking than his. There are also two wet suits draped on the top of hers. She has French pleated her hair so it drapes all down her back – bitch. I feel a rush of jealousy just in the fact that their whole beach spot looks so much more cooler than ours. We have no surf boards. Lou is sheltering herself under a giant-sized sun hat with dark shades and Faye is doing press ups. I'm not sure what it says about us but 'cool' doesn't spring to mind. I fiddle about, not knowing what to do or how to make us look cooler. I debate going to the Foster's tent and purchasing three pints but, given it's only eleven thirty in the morning and if I produce a pint in front of Lou right now she will vomit over my hand, I think again. As I look around I notice the stand saying, 'Surf School, train with the best, be the best'. That'll do, I think to myself. I saunter over to the stand and after five minutes I have booked into my first surf lesson with an Australian surf pro named Kit. He said a lot of stuff most of which I didn't understand but the words, ankle buster, backside, bitchin and cranking were definitely recognisable. Although for different reasons, I couldn't help but think of Mickey Vain…

After spending almost an entire ten minutes matching me to a surf board (I mean seriously, this guy was like some kind of horse whisperer for surf boards), I gave my size and was told to go change into my wetsuit. Now the truth is, I've never worn a wetsuit or anything similar in texture. It was only when I tried to pull the damn thing over my ankle that I realised this was no easy thing. I checked the suit to see if there were instructions. After a gruelling five minutes of pulling, swearing, sweating and making farting sounds, I somehow managed to get the suit on. I pulled it up to the top and used the extra-long zip which somehow really doesn't help, fasten it up at the back (they really should advertise the fact you need to be double jointed). I stand in front of the small mirror and notice the massive air-filled pocket just above my snatch. That can't be right, I think to myself. It's then that I remember all those films like Cagney and Lacey where the zip is at the front not the back. Fucking hell. I peel the suit off and start again, this time with the zip at the front. I walk out of the changing room straight onto the beach. I haven't pulled the zip right to the top, I show just enough cleavage to give the impression there is more than just squashed potatoes hiding in there.

I notice my instructor, Kit, is talking to someone, two people actually; Pete and Caz. Fuck. It's OK, I decide. I look hot. My muffin top is neatly tucked into my wet suit. I decide to take my sunglasses off and tuck them into the cleavage part of my wetsuit, so very Cagney and Lacey. As I saunter over, I can see they are looking. I have to say, I do feel pretty hot. Kit is smiling, a lot. Pete has taken a double take which has to be good, right, and Caz, well her face, I'm not quite sure how to read that. She looks like she is smirking.

"Jess," Kit takes hold of my hand. I like him already. He leans in towards my ear. I like this, it's like we are dating, yes, maybe we are dating. He whispers into my ear, "It goes the other way, gorgeous." I stand and wonder what he is talking about. Is it some euphemism and he knows Pete should belong to me? I take a moment but then realise, as I look at Kit, Pete and Caz that my wetsuit is on wrong. Caz is now not trying to hide the fact she is laughing. Fuckety fuck, fuck. Somehow, despite only knowing Kit for about ten milliseconds, he somehow feels my pain.

"It's the way they do it in Oz these days," he says. Pete makes a face that suggests, I don't quite believe what you are saying.

"So how do you know each other then," asks Pete.

"She's having her first…"

"First advanced lesson," I jump in – fuck knows why.

"Wow, that's great," says Pete. Even Caz looks impressed.

"Yeah, well, you know when you rip the waves, man, you know, they erm, really rip." Everyone is staring at me. Kit is looking at me. I know, I know, I say to myself. It's not like you can fake being a pro surfer, or even being able to surf. The proof is in the pudding but the reality is, it's a bacon sandwich, the pig is committed. I follow as Kit, Pete and Caz walk ahead towards the sea. Think, think Jess, how the hell am I going to get out of this. And then it happens, the twist on the child's sandpit, or the fake twist should I say. I cry out, oh, my ankle. Everyone turns. The kid looks at me, he has a bucket of water in his hand.

"You just stood on my sandcastle," he bellows, in a flood of tears.

"Ouch, my ankle, I twisted my ankle."

"You didn't," shouts the little shit. No one looks particularly convinced. I start limping over to them. "I can't weight bear on it," I pathetically add. "Damn it," I say, wanting this bullshit ordeal to be over with. "Guess no waves today." Caz has an 'mmmmm' face. She's not buying it. Kit looks quizzical, but I paid him up front though, so he is pretty cool with it.

What follows then is a gruelling fake five minutes of Kit applying ice to my perfectly normal feeling ankle and a concerned looking Pete, who genuinely appears concerned I may have hurt myself, again. As for Caz, she looks so pissed off it is actually making me smile, although I try to disguise it so she doesn't know my lie. Clearly, Pete's level of concern is more than just everyday concern – maybe? Pete and Caz eventually leave me after several reassurances that I am fine and I am sure it will be OK in a day or two, along with further reassurances about my nose which is still rather bruised.

I hobble back over to Faye and Lou and throw myself down on my towel. "That was quick," says Faye. Lou is asleep.

"Yeah, well, it only took about sixty seconds for me to make a complete tit of myself again." If I was hoping for compassion after sharing my humiliation with Faye, I couldn't have been more wrong. She looks really pissed off.

"That just isn't good enough, Jess, get it together. How are you going to win Pete back if you keep acting like a full on ditsy blond?"

"Hey," pipes up Lou.

"Jeez, sorry," I say with no sentiment. "I didn't realise it was so important to you." Faye glares at me. I lay back and hide my face with my arms. I need some time alone to deal with this.

"Look," shouts Faye. I wake up. I hadn't realised I had dropped off. "They are leaving."

"Who's leaving?" I ask.

"Pete and his tart."

"So," I say.

"So, you get your arse back over there and get that surfing lesson and make it a good one. You need to master this, Jess." Like a petulant child, I stomp off back to Kit.

"G'day, Jess. Has the foot healed?"

"Yeah, I, erm, think I just pulled something."

"Righto," says Kit. "Want that lesson now then?" he asks, slightly smirking.

"Yes, please." I say.

"Bonza." He throws me the wetsuit which I put on the correct way and we head to the ocean together.

Kit is an amazing teacher. He explains things so clearly and truly is an amazing surfer. It's such a shame all those skills were wasted on me. It was like something from a Carry On film. I hadn't realised there were so many skills involved from actually getting on the surf board (something which I struggled with, spending most of my time sprawled at the base of the board). They make it look so easy. I can honestly say, there is absolutely no way in my lifetime will I ever be able to kneel, stand and ride a wave. I am OK with this. The reality is that Pete will never fall for me now anyway. Why would he when he has the perfect woman on his arm? We decide to call it a day. Kit seems to have accepted this isn't going to happen.

Having peeled off my wetsuit, I step out of the hut back onto the beach. Standing there is Pete, alone, as in, without Caz.

"Not feeling the rip today, then?" he asks with a smirk on his face.

"Erm, well, no, as you can see, err, surfing and I are very much a work in progress," I reply, blushing that my lie has been discovered.

"Well you may have had more luck if your instructor didn't spend more time groping your arse than teaching you." Kit holds up his hands and grins. Bastard, I think.

"Come on," says Pete. "Grab your wetsuit, let's give it another go, a real lesson this time," he says, staring at Kit.

"Hey, that'll cost," says Kit. Pete raises his eyebrow. Ooh, he's sexy. "Fair enough," says Kit, looking a bit more disgruntled now. I contemplate protesting, not sure if my ego can face more humiliation today but then Pete is offering me some one on one time, alone, us two together and nothing but the ocean. Three minutes later, I fart my way out of the changing room, back in my wetsuit.

"Crikey that took some doing," I say. "Someone seriously has to invent a suit easier to get on." Pete smiles. He hands me the surf board I had been using with Kit.

"Come on," he says, guiding me towards the ocean.

"Just a minute, let me tell my friends." I walk over to Faye and Lou who seem to have acquired a posse. "I see it didn't take you long to recover," I say to Lou who is downing a pint.

"We're playing Bite the Bag." I don't need to ask. Faye is bent over with her arse cheeks in the air trying to pick up a plastic bag with her teeth in the sand. As she grabs it and stands up, her face is covered in sand, but she has the bag between the teeth. Some guys takes it off her and cuts a bit off the bag then lays it down for his turn.

"Listen," I say. "Don't hang about for me. I'm going to be kinda busy for a while," I say, nodding in the direction of Pete who is stood about three hundred yards away looking hot in his wetsuit.

"Go, Jess," shouts Lou.

"Sshh," I whisper. Faye nods a nod of approval.

"See you back at the pad," says Faye.

As Pete and I head to the ocean, I pluck up the courage to ask, "Where's Caz?"

"She's, err, having a nap." That's odd, I think to myself. I decide not to ask any more, perhaps they had a fight. Yes, I think to myself. They had a fight and now Pete has come back to me.

I try to keep up as Pete marches towards the ocean. That man is on a mission. I don't think he appreciates the challenge in walking in the sand and carrying a heavy board under your arm. If I thought this was going to be a romantic, flirty lesson, I can think again. Pete starts barking orders at me. He's barking orders at me to the point that this is becoming very serious indeed. I wasn't up for serious surfing. I was up for Pete laying on top of me on my board.

"Jess, Jess, are you paying attention?" he shouts. Fuck. Why is he being like this, I wonder. I'm starting to feel a bit pissed off. "No, not like that, like this," he says with a definite frustrated tone to his voice. Bloody hell. Where's Kit when you need him? My arse could really do with a massage.

"Right, now, now, Jess." Righto, I think. I'm getting tired of this fucker so I decide to just do it right so he will back off. I throw myself onto the board as the wave comes crashing behind me. Whoa. I glide towards the shore. That was it, I actually did it. I feel really proud of myself. I look to see if Pete approves. He is glaring.

"Did you see that?" I ask, beaming from ear to ear.

"Yes, that's what the kids do. We call it boogie boarding," he says. Well, excuse me, Mr Perfect Pants. "Come on, let's do it again," he says. He's lined up at the side of me. I copy him as he throws himself back onto the board. Amazingly, I manage to get myself to the top of the board and paddle back into the deeper water.

"Right, now when you see the wave, start paddling, then raise your knees and stand," he says. I look at him now. This definitely isn't funny. This is serious shit. I debate jumping off my surf board and dragging its sorry arse back to Kit but something inside me tells me to keep going. I'll show this fucker I can do it and then I will just grab my board and leave Mr Arsey Pants.

I see the wave as does Pete. "Start paddling," he says. I paddle, then somewhere from the depths of my ankles, I find the power to lift my knees. Somehow then, from my knees I almost jump up. Fuuuuuuckk. It all happens really quickly. One moment I am feeling like Mistress of the Universe, the next my mouth and throat are filled with water. It's like a bloody high-pressure hose has been connected to my mouth and I can't breathe. I am coughing. Choking... I realise I am looking up at the board floating above on the surface, I am under it. I must have fallen off. I start forcing my way back up, kicking, then suddenly there is a sharp pain just above my right ear and then nothing... darkness... everything is quiet.

I'm on a bouncy castle being thrown up, up into the air. The bouncing feels exhilarating, like someone is making me bounce harder and harder, WTF! I start to come out of it and am coming around. I start to cough. Blurrrgghhh. I'm startled. I think I just threw up something. I realise my eyes are closed. I have no idea where I am. As I slowly open my eyes, I see these deep watery blue eyes looking down on me and something heavy pummelling my chest. Pete is directly on top of me. His hands are pounding my chest. What the hell happened?

"Jess, Jess, you with me?" I try to nod but have no movement in my limbs. I am paralysed. Fuck! Then I notice it's not just Pete, there is a whole fucking crowd surrounding me, gawping, open-mouthed like goldfish. I try to sit up. Pete helps me.

"You OK?" he asks. He looks shit scared.

"I'm fine, I think," I say. Just then I hear a siren. Within seconds, I am choking on sand as an ambulance pulls up next to me. What the hell, who's hurt? Two paramedics shift Pete out of the way and start fussing about me with blood pressure pumps and all kinds of crap. They're here for me? Shit!

"I'm fine," I announce, waving them out of my face. I focus on Pete. He looks like that kid that just pissed his pants in the playground. After flapping my arms around wildly, the paramedics eventually withdraw.

"Best take you down to get you checked over."

"Jeez, no, I'm fine." I say.

"Jess, listen to the medics."

"I'm fine," I say. "What happened exactly?"

"You fell off, you got hit on the head with the surf board." I nod. It's all coming back to me now.

"I stood up," I announce, to everyone around me. No one appears to be impressed – bastards. I stand up. Everyone hovers around me like I'm about to fall. "I'm fine," I insist. I move towards Pete.

"I stood up," I say.

"I know," he says, "because I made you." I don't understand.

"You didn't make me, I did it myself, didn't I?" I begin to wonder whether he somehow grabbed my legs and made me stand. I'm fairly certain it was all me.

"No, Jess. I was being an arse. I forced you to stand and look what happened?" He looks forlorn. By now, the observers are starting to disperse. Bored probably, that I didn't die. After many,

many more reassurances, the paramedics leave after I promise to head straight to A&E should I in anyway feel peculiar.

By the time everyone leaves, its dusk and there is just Pete and I on the beach. We start to head back towards Kit's beach hut.

"So, just why were you being such an arse?" I ask. I figure since I nearly died, a question like this wouldn't kill me. Pete stops. He sits down on the sand. I stand there trying to decide if I, too, should sit. I decide to sit. I feel like I'm walking on a cloud as it is.

"The thing is, Jess, Caz and I, well, you know, I thought I was happy with her, I thought she was it but then I saw you. Why the fuck did you have to show up?" I'm slightly taken aback. I wasn't expecting this.

"I just came on holiday with my mates," I say. "I couldn't afford Ibiza, it's way too expensive."

"It's a rhetorical question, Jess. I thought I had found the one but seeing you, well, it made me doubt everything."

"Jeez, Pete, I really don't think you can blame me. We met like what, seven years ago. You fingered me, so what."

"Oh, OK, so it's just me then, it's just me who connected." He starts to stand. He's angry again. Crapsticks. That's not what I meant. My protective shield is up because he has a girlfriend. I need to dilute it.

"Pete, Peter," I say, standing. Jeez, he is so intolerant. He stops but doesn't say anything. "It wasn't you, just you, you have no idea how many times I dreamt about something like this. You know it took me like a whole month to speak to my mother again after she changed the number. You were it. You were the real deal, the one, him, my first true love. I had your name sprawled everywhere. I somehow thought if I wrote your name enough, you would appear. My heart broke, Pete. It was crazy how I felt

176

for you but then here you are, you turn up, you're in love, you almost break my nose with a baguette and I'm like, shit, did that just happen? And now you tell me you have feelings for me. I do too, Pete. You do something to me." As I say this, my bowels start to rumble. He looks at me. I look at him. We stand there, looking at each other. He wipes the dried blood off my head and strokes my face.

I think we are about to kiss, that is until I hear, "Peter, where the fuck have you been? You said you were going to get some wax for your board – that was over two hours ago." Pete closes his eyes as Caz marches up behind him.

"Hi," I say. She ignores me. She stands between Pete and me.

"Peter, are you going to answer me? What have you been doing and why is SHE here?" Pete still doesn't answer. I need to help him out.

"I had an accident in the water. Pete saw me and helped that's all," I say. She looks at me and I notice she sees the cut above my ear. She's not happy but her face becomes softer.

"Always the hero, aren't you, darling?" she says, snuggling into him. I want to bash her out the way with my surf board.

"Well, then," I say. "So, thanks again Pete. Who knows what might have happened if you hadn't have been there… so, I guess I will leave you guys to it." As the words come out of my lips, I feel a lump rising in the back of my throat. Say something, Pete, I think to myself. Say, "Wait, Jess, don't go," but there is nothing. He says nothing, so I start to walk back to the hut. I daren't turn around for fear they will see the tears rolling down my face.

Then suddenly, "Jess." I turn, quickly wiping the tears from my eyes. "You sure you are OK?" he asks.

"Perfect, I'm perfect," I say and keep walking. So, that's it. He's gone again and this time it feels like it's for good. How the hell am I going to get over this? How do I explain this to Faye?

No one is in the apartment when I get back. Probably a good thing, I think to myself, so I can sit and mope on my own for a bit. I grab a beer out of the fridge and go and sit in the back yard. It's carnage out back. The yard is packed with blond surfer-looking dudes. Somewhere amongst them is Faye and Lou.

"What the hell happened now?" shouts Faye when she sees me.

"I stood up, but not for long." I don't need to explain any more, it's obvious what happened.

"Where's Pete?" asks Faye.

"With Caz," I reply. She looks at me then places her arm around my shoulder.

"Come on, come and meet the Aussies." I decide getting shit faced will definitely help numb the pain in both my ear and heart.

The rest of the holiday passes by in a blur. A mixture of too much sea salt, Fosters, Whimpey burgers and Aussies. I don't see Pete again after the surfing incident. Not that I wasn't on Fistral Beach every day, looking for him, he just never showed up. Caz probably banned him.

I throw my suitcase onto the train. Faye and Lou are both on the platform having one more goodbye snog to a mop of bleached blond hair. I'm pleased they both had a holiday romance. My brief encounter with an Aussie called Drew lasted just the one night. Seems being a hot Australian surfer gets you a lot of female action and this Australian wasn't going to spend more than one night with the one girl. Although to be fair to him, he did ask if I wanted to join him with Sasha for a threesome, but I politely declined. I'm not ready for that yet but it is on my bucket list.

As I sit watching Faye and Lou saying their goodbyes, I begin to think about Pete and what could have been. I start to daydream that he would appear at the station. I close my eyes to carry on the daydream and promise myself I will never think about him again once the train leaves the station.

I open my eyes to a banging sound. Faye is banging on the window of the train. What is she doing? She is going to get me kicked off. She's mouthing something, it looks like "heat". What's she on about? I mouth back "heat"? She's nodding furiously and pointing. I look to where she is pointing and then I see him, Pete. It's Pete, not heat. What's Pete doing here? I make a double take. How the chuff can he have got out of my head and onto the platform. I watch as he walks towards the door of the train. The next thing, he is in the carriage, standing in front of me.

"Jess, thank god I found you. Don't go. Stay with me."

"What?" I ask, not knowing what to say.

"Don't go," he says, "stay down here with me."

"But," is all I can manage.

"I broke up with Caz. She's on a coach back to Manchester. I realised it wasn't going to work with her, she's just not, not you." Faye and Lou are now on the train.

"You need to decide, Jess. The train is about to leave." I look at Faye and Lou. They are smiling. That's it, without a second thought I grab my suitcase. Pete takes it off me and we walk off the train together. I can't believe it. He came back for me. We stand on the platform. He's smiling at me then he leans in and gives me the biggest, wettest snog of my life. This is it. Every inch of my body tells me that this is it. This is the man I am going to spend the rest of my life with. I could never imagine being without him, I'd have to kill myself.

Chapter Thirteen

I take a step towards the edge. My heart is racing. My head is saying pull back, but my body ignores it and steps forward. I can hear people shouting from below. I try to block out the noise and instead focus on the task ahead. I know what needs to be done. Without further hesitation, I step off the edge. I am dropping. My scream echoes all around me but then I stop and the only sound I can hear is the air, like chimes ringing in my ears as I fall. My heart race has gone into overdrive. I try to calm it, but it matches the speed at which I fall, faster and faster. My stomach is in knots for fear of what is at the bottom. Will I feel anything? Will it hurt? In one mighty throw, I am pulled back and tossed back into the air until down I come crashing again.

"Whoa, that was awesome," I shout. I am springing up and down like a yoyo. Two hands then grab my legs and pull me to the ground. I have stopped springing but I can still feel the bounce in my body. Pete is stood there, smiling from ear to ear. I feel exhilarated, happy and free. I did it. I actually did it. I throw my arms around Pete.

"I did it, Pete. I never thought I could." He hugs me tightly.

"My little dare devil. You truly are nuts." I proudly put on the t-shirt he has bought me, '**I survived! Brisbane Bungee, Australia**.' This was more than just a bungee jump, this was a full-on bounce into the next chapter and I couldn't wait to see what happened next.